BLESSED NICHOLAS POSTGATE

MARTYR OF THE MOORS

NICHOLAS RHEA

GRACEWING

First published in England in 2012
by
Gracewing
2 Southern Avenue
Leominster
Herefordshire HR6 0QF
United Kingdom
www.gracewing.co.uk

ISBN 978 085244 785 7

Typeset by Gracewing

Cover design by Bernardita Peña Hurtado,
incorporating detail from the stained glass window
in St Hedda's church, Egton Bridge.

CONTENTS

PREFACE

Recording the life and times of Father Nicholas Postgate DD, who was born more than 400 years ago, can never be easy. There is very little recorded information although a handful of books and several articles have been written. An important early article was by Dom Bede Camm in his *Forgotten Shrines* (1910), followed by Father David Quinlan's book and serialisation *The Father Postgate Story* published by the Whitby Gazette (1967), then Monica Ventress's article in her book *A Little about Littlebeck* (2009). Father Hugh Aveling, a monk of Ampleforth Abbey researched his life in considerable depth whilst popular books dedicated to the martyr include the CTS pamphlet *Ven. Nicholas Postgate* (1928), Elizabeth Hamilton's *Priest of the Moors* (1980) and Christopher David Lyth's *Father Postgate and the Catholic Struggle* (2008).

Many other articles and features about the North York Moors, and indeed some topographical books, have included references to Father Postgate's life and work, most of them within the last half century. However, in those accounts, his work as a chaplain some distance from the North York Moors seems to have been largely ignored. In fact his mission as a chaplain in other parts of Yorkshire occupied him for about twice the length of time he was a priest on Blackamoor. See the map on page x.

However, a complete account of his life is impossible due to the passage of time but also because of the secrecy of his work and the lack of available evidence.

Despite this, it is possible to establish a fairly strong background from surviving records but it was during my recent research into the life of Blessed Nicholas Postgate that I discovered something hitherto unknown to me.

I learned that the well-documented home of his parents—James and Margaret Postgate—was within some 300 or 400 yards of the house where I was born. My elevated home overlooked that part of Egton that is still known as Kirkdale, with Kirkdale Banks just across the River Esk below our house.

That revelation was totally unexpected (I was only a few months old when I left my place of birth) and the coincidence will be will be explained within these pages, if only to show this was not contrived! However, it led me to decide that the theme of this book should be my own journey of discovery in the footsteps of the Blessed Nicholas Postgate as I attempted to learn more about him, his ministry and the landscape in which he worked. This book, therefore marks a very personal journey.

This, then, is the story of a Yorkshire lad growing up in a remote rural parish in the midst of the North York Moors, earning a prestigious Doctor of Divinity degree at the English College at Douai University, winning the trust, respect and love of hundreds of people as a priest, and then in 1679, suffering death as a martyr on the Knavesmire near York.

Father Postgate, as we 'locals' all called him, was beatified in Rome by Pope John Paul II on 22nd November, 1987, together with a further 84 English martyrs.

AUTHOR'S NOTE: In its bottom right corner, the map on p. 4 shows Kirkdale Banks. It is bordered by Stonegate Beck where it joins the River Esk (MR 780068). The three black dots beside the path are houses (p. 16 et seq), one of which was the Postgate family home. This is probably the only visible evidence of the martyr's home and place of birth.

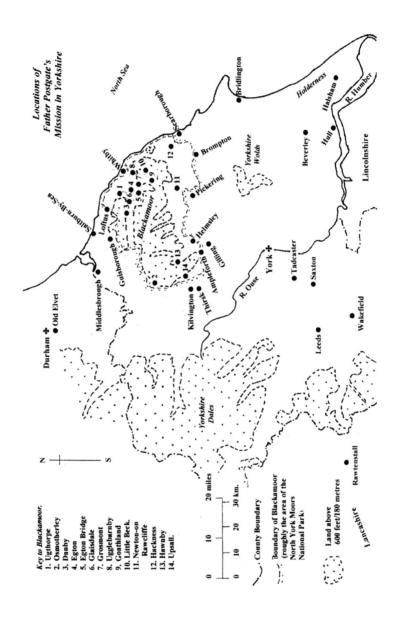

Locations of
*Father Postgate's
Mission in Yorkshire*

Key to Blackamoor.
1. Ugthorpe
2. Osmotherley
3. Danby
4. Egton
5. Egton Bridge
6. Glaisdale
7. Grosmont
8. Ugglebarnby
9. Goathland
10. Little Beck
11. Newton-on
   Rawcliffe
12. Hackness
13. Hawnby
14. Upsall.

. . County Boundary

: . : Boundary of Blackamoor
     (roughly the area of the
     North York Moors
     National Park).

Land above
600 feet/180 metres

CHAPTER 1

Childhood

WHILE FOLLOWING THE footsteps of Father Postgate we will not discover a great deal about his childhood although we may learn more about the district in which he grew up. However, there are interesting arguments about his *place* of birth—it may not have been Egton Bridge as tradition suggests. There is information about his parents and siblings but little about how he occupied his time or the interests he followed. Likewise, we cannot be sure of his physical appearance, although hand-relics at Ampleforth and Durham suggest he was small with delicate hands. His escape route from the Mass House (Chapter 6) also suggests a small man. Even his true age and family circumstances are open to argument. In short, Father Postgate's early life maintains a mystery. The following pages highlight what I have learned and it is almost certain that more will be discovered in future years, the most likely sources being letters and wills that have survived.

1. Father Postgate's parentage and family

It is not in doubt that his father was James Postgate but the chief question is: was his mother Jane or Margaret? And precisely how many people lived in his parents' home? Indeed, could Margaret and Jane be the same person? Both are described as widows in the 1605 and 1611 Recusant Returns for Egton. Both are also said to be the mother of Nicholas.

First, let us examine claims that Jane was his mother. The Civil Recusants Return for Egton Parish in 1604 lists a Jane Postgate, widow, living at Kirkedale (sic) and there is an addendum to state she was the mother of Nicholas. Jane's name as his mother is supported by Bede Camm,[1] and is also given in Edward Peacock's 1604 list of Catholics in Yorkshire.

Peacock called her: 'Jane Posgate (sic) of Kirkdale, a widow' adding that those Postgates were clearly relatives of Nicholas. However, the exact degree of that relationship 'will probably remain forever uncertain.'[2] Camm adds that the father of Nicholas Postgate was apparently the son of William Postgate of Kirkdale. In other words, William (the teacher) was Nicholas' grandfather. He adds that the mother of Nicholas, namely Jane according to him, was living at Kirkdale in 1604 and writes, 'Jane Postgate, a widowe, doth keep in her house William Postgate her father, a recusant who teacheth children and also Marmaduke Petch and Jane Smallwood, recusants.' So was Jane the aunt of Nicholas? The sister of James perhaps?

According to Peacock's interpretation of the Recusants Lists, Jane was possibly the daughter of William, or alternatively 'Postgate' may have been her married name—which was not impossible. In that case she would be his daughter-in-law. But if that was the case, who was her husband?

So was Jane a widow or a spinster? And was Jane's father truly William who was also father of James? The term *father* was sometimes used to describe an elderly, venerable or respected man even if he was not related. Or was he really her father-in-law? The use of commas in that sentence can lead to confusion too, but we may presume that Grandad William was himself a recusant who taught recusants' children. So was it he who gave the young Nicholas such a splendid education, fine enough for him to be later accepted by the English College at Douai University?

Jane may have been thought the mother of Nicholas because there was a Jane in the Postgate family who lived at Dean Hall near Littlebeck. Curiously, that particular Jane's husband was also called James and this led to a belief that Nicholas was born at Dean Hall, not far from Red Barns where he was later arrested.

It now appears that the Dean Hall family of Postgates lived there in Elizabethan times although Nicholas was born during the final years of that reign.

Queen Elizabeth I died in 1603 and Nicholas is thought to have been born around 1600. In fact, Edward Peacock records numerous 'Postgates' in that area which is collectively known as Eskdaleside. It was once thought that the mystery of Margaret and Jane would never be resolved but a legal document discovered by Father David Quinlan[3] confirmed Margaret Postgate's role as the mother of Nicholas. It also stated his father was called James. James died in 1602 when Nicholas was a toddler, so at only 23 years of age Margaret became a widow with four young children.[4] We do not know the name or gender of the fourth—perhaps Nicholas had a sister whose details are not recorded?

The document discovered by Father Quinlan, a former parish priest of Egton Bridge, was a Conveyance dated 1620 for a farm or small-holding worked by (sic) 'Margaret Poscatt of Kirkdale-Banckes'. This provides evidence that the family lived (at least for a time) at Kirkdale Banks which may have been the site of Kirkdale House, sometimes known as Kirk House. The 1604 Recusants List also showed Ninian and Marian Smithson living at Kirkdale Banks, plus a servant called Isabel Holmes. They would probably be neighbours of the Postgates. I believe there were three un-named dwellings at Kirkdale Banks, one of which was home to the Post-gates (see the 1636 map, on p. 4). It also seems that modest dwellings were not then named—they were identified by their location and/or their occupants' names.

Map of the Lordship of Egton in 1636[5]

In support of the Conveyance found by Father Quinlan, the family tree of Nicholas Postgate is given in Margarent Urquhart's article 'Was Christopher Simpson a Jesuit?'.[6] This states that James Postgate, the father of Nicholas, lived at Kirkdale Banks, Egton and it also confirms that James married Margaret Watson.

Further confirmation of that marriage is that during his secret missionary work Nicholas used his mother's maiden name of 'Watson' as an alias. Margaret Postgate died in 1624, probably aged 44 or 45. There were three sons, Matthew, William and Nicholas, and it is recorded that Matthew married a woman called Elizabeth. In this family tree, there is no reference to a sister or other brother for Nicholas.

Already it will be seen that Kirkdale and Kirkdale Banks have been mentioned several times but I must stress, at this point, that Kirkdale Banks was NOT in Egton *Bridge* and neither was Kirkdale. The Egton map dated 1636 shows otherwise and I will later explain its relevance.

From the Civil Recusants Returns for Egton (1611) it appears that Margaret, by then a widow, moved house because a servant girl called Anne Postgate, aged 18, was working for Margaret Postgate at West Banks, Egton. I don't think there was a change of house because West Banks was a settlement at Kirkdale Banks—it was a hamlet comprising three dwellings as shown on my 1636 map. Kirkdale Banks was the name of the parcel of land upon which West Banks stood and today a farm called West Banks exists at that location, namely south-east corner of the former Kirkdale Banks whose name no longer exists. The names of both Kirkdale Banks and West Banks appear in the Recusants Lists of that period, although I believe those former buildings have been incorporated within the present farm and its outbuildings. Recycling old buildings in this way was a common practice on those moors in the 18th and 19th centuries.

In the July 1614 Recusants List, Margaret Postgate is recorded aged 40 and the mother of Nicholas. An addendum suggests the scribe may have estimated some recorded ages! If this was the mother of Nicholas, she would have been around 35 at the time of the 1614 returns so perhaps 40 was a reasonable estimate.

However, she could have moved from house to house within a small area—quite likely in such a compact rural area among friends and relations.

A woman called Margaret Postgate is recorded as living at Kirkdale House, Egton (not Egton Bridge) but another Margaret Postgate, a widow, is shown on the Recusants Lists for West Banks, Egton in 1605. My documentary researches and visits to the locality provide evidence that Kirkdale House, West Banks, Egton Banks and Kirkdale Banks were all within a very compact area of what used to be the parish of Egton. I think the two references relate to the same woman because Egton Banks was part of Kirkdale Banks and individual houses were not identified.

Relations of the Postgates included other families in the vicinity and they were related by marriage to the Simpsons (Chapter 2). Christopher Simpson's brother (or uncle) Robert, married Alice, the daughter of Ralph Postgate.[7] The Simpsons' home was at Westonby, half a mile or so from Kirkdale Banks. This adds support to the evidence that this area of Egton, around one square mile, was teeming with recusants.

So what else is known about Margaret Postgate? She appeared on the Recusants Lists for Egton and is thought to have paid the 10 shilling fine (50p) imposed on the 13-year old Nicholas when he was a member of the Simpson Players of Egton (see chapter 2). At that time, a schoolmaster's annual wage was about £4 so a ten shilling fine was huge, being half of £1. When Margaret died in 1624 the administration of her Will was conducted on 15th April that year and her estate at *Kirkdale Banks* was valued at £40, a considerable sum at that time. Her heir was her eldest son, Matthew. I have highlighted Kirkdale Banks to stress it is not Kirkdale House at Egton Bridge which, by tradition, was the birthplace of Nicholas Postgate.

At the time of his mother's death, Nicholas Postgate was overseas training to be a priest and there is no record of him returning to England to attend her funeral. Catholics were then buried in Protestant churchyards without the Catholic liturgy.

Mrs Postgate's place of burial is not known but it would surely be in the graveyard at the head of Kirkdale, Egton. That graveyard still exists beside Egton Mortuary Chapel which stands on the site of Egton's ancient Catholic Church of St Hilda. Her resting place may have been an unmarked but consecrated Catholic grave and she may have been buried there secretly.

Her middle son William left Egton Bridge to live in Oxfordshire and married Joanna Mylott, also a Catholic. It is claimed by Elizabeth Hamilton[8] that they became the parents of Ralph Postgate (born 1648) who became a distinguished Jesuit priest and twice Rector of the Venerable English College in Rome. Like his Uncle Nicholas, he was also educated at Douai but died in Rome in 1718. However, according to the CTS pamphlet, *Ven. Nicholas Postgate*[9] it is not certain whether Ralph Postgate was a relative of the Egton family.[10] However, a Ralph Postgate does appear in Margaret Urquhart's article about Christopher Simpson.[11] That presents another mystery in the life of Nicholas Postgate.

In his research for the 1928 CTS pamphlet, Father William Storey, the parish priest of Egton Bridge, was assisted by a man who lived in poverty at Egton. He was Will Ward who had spent a lifetime gathering information, memorabilia and papers relating to Father Postgate. When I asked the Librarian at Ushaw College (before it was due to close in September, 2011 for its transfer to Oscott) whether he stocked any documents relating to Father Postgate, he assured me there was none in the College library but there were copies of three letters, not originals, of correspondence dating 1707/8 between Ralph Postgate, SJ, and Andrew Giffard. Despite some detailed research, it remains uncertain whether this Ralph Postgate had any links with the martyr, Nicholas, although this Ralph was a Jesuit.

To add a little more to the difficulty with names at that time, in the district around Egton there were—and still are—many ways of spelling and pronouncing Postgate. They include Poskitt, Poskett, Posket, Poscatt, Posgate and Postgayt, the latter being the martyr's own spelling as it appeared in his signature in a book on display at St Hedda's Church, Egton Bridge. Other phonetic-based spellings of the name frequently occur but Postgate is not used solely as a family surname.

It is also a place-name whilst within reach of Egton there is Postgate Farm at Glaisdale and the Postgate Cross on the moors above Whitby (MR 919044). Neither is thought to be named in honour of the martyr. The prefix *post* means exactly that, usually in the form of a stone pillar, and *gate* is derived from from the Old Norse *gata* meaning a street or road (cf. *Gasse* in German, a lane). Many streets in ancient Yorkshire towns, for example York, Richmond, Whitby and others contain streets which end with the suffix *gate,* a word with Scandinavian origins. Postgate therefore means a road or street with a post or posts.

So who was the mother of Nicholas Postgate? I am sure it was Margaret—after all, he used her maiden name as an alias.

2. Nicholas Postgate's date of birth

There is considerable uncertainty about Father Postgate's date of birth. The lack of clarity persisted throughout his long life, although it is widely believed he was born in 1599/1600. Edward Peacock says he was born about the end of the 16th century[12] whilst Father Storey in his *'Ven. Nicholas Postgate' (1928)* suggests the date of 1596.[13] In the style of Father Postgate's time, this would be written as either 1595/1596 or 1596/1597 thus giving rise to other suggested dates for his birth, namely 1595 or 1597, depending upon which month he was born. The most widely accepted birth date is 1599/1600 but this does *not* suggest a choice of two years.

In his time, this method of writing the date covered one period of twelve successive months—an entire year. The reason is that New Year's Day then occurred on March 25, known in short as Lady Day and more formally as The Annunciation. This is when The Virgin Mary received news that she would bear a Son called Jesus and to distinguish it from other days dedicated to her, it was sometimes known as St Mary's Day in Lent. In England it was also the beginning of the legal year and the date upon which rents were due or new tenancies were arranged and old ones terminated. March 25 was therefore a very important date.

Curiously, Bede Camm does not suggest a date of birth for Nicholas Postgate but 1599/1600 is put forward by Father David Quinlan who undertook detailed research into the martyr's life, and who helped me in my early writing career. However, Elizabeth Hamilton, emulating Peacock in her *The Priest of the Moors* (1980) decided to be imprecise by stating 'Nicholas Postgate was born about the year 1600.'[14] In attempting to determine his date of birth, we can say that if he had been born between March 25 and December 31 that year, his date of birth would have been recorded as 1600.

If his birthday was in January, February or any date before March 25 of that year, then his birthday would be recorded as 1599. In calculating his age, therefore, there is a possible discrepancy of at least one year.

Furthermore, any modern calculations may be affected by England's rather late adoption of the Gregorian calendar. When it became evident that the four seasons were not corresponding with their calendar dates, Pope Gregory XIII decided to correct the error.

The calendar then in use, (the Julian calendar named after Julius Caesar), resulted in the spring equinox, which occurred on 25th March at the time of Caesar, falling much earlier in 1582. In that year it arrived on 11th March. Caesar's calculations based on 365.25 days per year were proven faulty and by the time of Pope Gregory the Julian calendar was in error by 11 minutes and 14 seconds *per year*. Gregory corrected this by first removing 11 days from the calendar in October 1582; therefore October 5 was re-designated October 15. Gregory's final calculation was to include a leap year once every four years, except when the year-date was exactly divisible by 400, like in 1600 and 2000. It was the Gregorian calendar that introduced 1ˢᵗ January as New Year's Day—but not until 1752 in England. Thus the calendar and the seasons began to co-operate with much more precision.

Nonetheless, Gregory's new calendar caused a mighty rumpus with some people believing their lives had been shortened by 11 days, and with some religious festivals being held on the day they would have occurred had there *not* been a new calendar. In parts of England, there was stubborn resistance to the change and we still hear references to Old Christmas Day, Old Barnaby Day, Old Martinmas Day and so forth. Pope Gregory's calculations meant that the spring equinox of 21 March 1583 corresponded with his new calendar.

However, although Catholic countries had adopted the Gregorian calendar in 1582, it was not adopted by Protestant England until 1752, almost two hundred years later because the authorities were said to have suspected some kind of Papist plot.

All this compounds the uncertainty about the precise date of Nicholas Postgate's birth and sadly, Egton's parish registers will not establish his age because they date from 1622. In any case, the Postgate children were secretly baptised by a Catholic priest instead of a Church of England minister.[15]

Problems with his date of birth will be shown in the following chapters but it does seem that the compromise of *'around 1600'* is most acceptable.

3. Nicholas Postgate's place of birth

Determining the place of birth for Father Postgate has proved a most difficult task, despite the most widely acknowledged site being Kirkdale House, Egton Bridge.

Egton Bridge is a beautiful small village in North Yorkshire's Eskdale some eight miles inland from Whitby. However, despite an absence of documentary proof, although supported by years of tradition, Kirkdale House, Egton Bridge continues to be the generally accepted location of the martyr's birth, However, my research suggests otherwise because the family home was at Kirkdale Banks, Egton.

The reasons for my argument will follow but there are other contenders so I will deal with them first.

(a) Dean Hall, Ugglebarnby near Littlebeck

Father Hugh Aveling, OSB, a monk of Ampleforth Abbey otherwise known as the author, J. C. H. Aveling, states in his *Northern Catholics* (1966) that Nicholas Postgate was born at Dean Hall near Littlebeck, the son of a wealthy farmer. Littlebeck is a tiny community six miles east of Egton Bridge and in Elizabethan times, a family called Postgate did live at Dean Hall. Amongst them was a James Postgate, a recusant with a wife called Margery,[16] and in common with other Postgates of that area, they may have been related to the Postgates of Egton.

The fact that Nicholas' family appeared able to afford the recusant fines or even possibly make a contribution towards his eventual tuition at The English College at Douai does suggest a degree of wealth. However, no other source has suggested he was born at Dean Hall.

As a matter of interest, Dean Hall is only a mile or so from Red Barn, Littlebeck where Father Postgate was arrested whilst baptising a baby.

To complicate matters, there were other 'James Postgates' living nearby at Sleights, Goathland and Eskdaleside whilst yet another James was in the employ of John Constable at Burton Constable in the East Riding of Yorkshire.[17]

(b) Newbiggin Hall

This is a large farmhouse still standing between Egton and Aislaby and when I was a child at Egton Bridge Catholic Primary school, a story was in circulation that Newbiggin Hall was the site of Father Postgate's birth. There was absolutely no documentary proof although Father Postgate did visit the house in later life, probably to celebrate Mass or for some other private or professional reason. I feel that the story was nothing more than a local rumour.

It is possible that this story arose due to some confusion with Biggin House, Ugthorpe just over two miles away across open country. The name of Biggin House cropped up at Father Postgate's trial at York Assizes when a witness, Elizabeth Baxter, gave evidence that he had celebrated Mass at Biggin House. As a matter of record, it has also been claimed that he was arrested at Biggin House and not Red Barn at Ugglebarnby.[18]

(c) Kirkdale House, Egton Bridge

Although widely accepted as Nicholas Postgate's birth-place, I doubt whether Kirkdale House ever existed in Egton Bridge. It does not appear on the Recusants Lists at that location and in 1636 that traditional locality was not called Kirkdale. Nearby fields were: Broad Field, Woody Field and Frank Close with Low Wood Intake being the largest. But in 1636 there were several un-named buildings beyond the bridge when heading towards Goathland and Rosedale.

By tradition, Kirkdale House was said to be on the left, immediately across the bridge. Today however, (2011–2012) a Kirkdale Cottage stands near the traditional site but it is a modern structure and cannot be associated with the martyr. So what are the arguments in favour of the martyr's birthplace being at Kirkdale House, Egton Bridge?

Bede Camm states 'Nicholas Postgate was born at Kirkdale House in the parish of Egton near Whitby.'[19] That appears to be very clear but on the following page he writes, 'Kirkdale, or Kirk House, our martyr's birthplace, stood near Egton Bridge.' He does not provide a source for that information—he may have relied on three centuries of local tradition—now four centuries of local tradition!

It should be stressed that Egton and Egton Bridge are quite separate communities more than a mile apart—and there was a bridge in Egton Bridge, hence its name. It was, and still is, a road bridge that crosses the River Esk near Egton Manor. In Father Postgate's time it was the site of Bridgeholme Green and home of the aristocratic Catholic family of Smiths. It was this family that did so much to keep the Catholic faith alive on the surrounding moors, and it is possible that their role led to the area's wide reputation as a hot-bed of papists.

Other bridges have stood on that site and a modern one is there today with a second one near Egton Bridge railway station. If, therefore, old records referred to *Egton Bridge,* did they mean the hamlet or merely an area close to the bridge?

Let's take a closer look at the case for Kirkdale House at Egton Bridge.

(i) A cattle shed

When I attended Egton Bridge primary school more than 70 years ago, all the pupils were proudly shown Father Postgate's place of birth in the corner of a field near the bridge at Egton Bridge. It was nothing more than a pile of dressed stones.

They were on the *left* when heading out of the village towards Goathland and Rosedale and very close to the river bank. I can recall the stones looking like the remains of a tumbledown and rather meagre dry stone wall. So were those stones truly the remains of Kirkdale House or were they merely the remains of a sheep shelter, cattle shed or indeed a tumbledown dry stone wall? As an adult re-considering that tumble of stones, I doubt they could have been the remains of an entire house—there were too few but we must accept that, over many years, most would have been removed or stolen. Furthermore, that particular site was far too close to the River Esk for comfort. Any dwelling house would have been on higher ground away from the unstable moods of the river although it is on record that some remains of Kirkdale House were visible at this locality in 1838, described as 'little more than a cattle shed'.[20]

Was it the same pile of stones we had admired a century or so later? Or were they the remains of its lower walls? Stone-built houses were for the well-off people or aristocrats. At that time, ordinary folk made do with wattle and daub. In short, we had no idea where those stones had come from.

However, this locality is strongly believed to be the birthplace of Nicholas Postgate and that assurance persisted long before my schoolmates and I appeared on the scene. So could it be true? Or has it acquired that status due to little more than rumour and tradition with little or no supporting evidence? Father David Quinlan wrote in the *Whitby Gazette* of 17th February 1967, 'Immediately beyond the bridge, behind a barred gate across a track which was once a road, lie the foundations of the very small cottage known as Kirkdale House, the birthplace of Ven. Nicholas Postgate in 1599.' That bold statement appears to seal the matter.

It was supported by the CTS pamphlet *Ven. Nicholas Postgate* (1928), whose author was also a priest at Egton Bridge.

He wrote, 'Nicholas Postgate was born in 1596 (sic) at Kirkdale House in the parish of Egton'.[21] He does not state 'Egton Bridge' but adds, 'The house was *probably* situated in the village itself, near the bridge' and he adds that the site was 'on the left a little beyond the bridge.' Elizabeth Hamilton also exercises some caution by writing, 'Kirkdale House at Egton Bridge is generally *assumed* to be the place where Nicholas Postgate was born.'[22] The italics are mine.

The 1928 CTS pamphlet *Ven. Nicholas Postgate* stated that the remains were 'literally a cattle shed in 1838.'[23] Like the stones I saw as a child, those remains have vanished. That is not surprising but I do wonder whether the home of an ordinary rural dweller would then have been built of stones, or would it have been wattle and daub with a thatched roof, albeit with stones around the bases of the walls? And would it have had foundations?

So far as I can tell, the location of Kirkdale House at Egton Bridge does not appear to be supported by real evidence and I wonder how much of that old tradition is based on nothing more than an unexplained, convenient and enduring pile of stones?

In the late summer of 2011, whilst I was researching and writing these notes, a team of archaeologists from York University had earlier been invited to excavate the likely site of Kirkdale House at Egton Bridge but at a meeting of the Postgate Society on 5th May 2011, the Dowager Marchioness of Normanby, initiator and patron of that research, reported that the results were likely to be inconclusive. No geophysical evidence of a building was found and even if such evidence did emerge, it would not prove the building had been Kirkdale House or the birthplace of Nicholas Postgate.

My own research led me to the North Yorkshire County Records Office at Northallerton on 28th July 2011 when I examined and enlarged a copy of a map. It covers an area of The Lordship of Egton in the County of York, 1636.[24] It includes both Egton and Egton Bridge but does not feature the name of Kirkdale in Egton Bridge, although the name does appear in locations at Egton. However, I found indications of seven unnamed buildings around Egton Bridge with some along the road from the bridge towards Goathland and close to the traditional site of Kirkdale House—but not upon it.

So does this suggest that Father Postgate may have been born elsewhere?

(d) The significance of Kirkdale Banks

Although the name of Kirkdale Banks appeared in Recusants Lists and other documents, its significance and even its location have apparently been overlooked. It is not shown on modern maps and, to my knowledge, the location has never been suggested as a possible birthplace for our martyr. Perhaps it was assumed that Kirkdale Banks was an area of Egton Bridge? If that was the case, it would sound like a very suitable location for Kirkdale House.

Here I must question whether small cottages of the type thought to have been occupied by the Postgate family would carry names. Certainly large dwellings such as farms, halls, manors and palaces carried names, but even in my own lifetime, country cottages were often un-named. I recall buying one in 1967 locally known as Miss Worthy's Cottage because Miss Worthy had once lived there.

However, in discussing Kirkdale Banks, I can state that the assumed and traditional site of Kirkdale House, Egton Bridge was upon land that could be described as a bank. That is the local term for a hill or piece of sloping ground. One of my maps, a copy of Sheet 13 (published by David and Charles) but originally the work of Ordnance Survey in 1843, clearly shows Bridgeholme Green and Egton Bridge but no Kirkdale Banks at Egton Bridge. Also, the copy of my 1636 map shows Brig-Holme Green Farm but no Kirkdale references in Egton Bridge.

However, two other sources, quite independently, have placed both Nicholas Postgate's mother and his father at Kirkdale Banks, Egton. One is Father David Quinlan who wrote in 'The Father Postgate story'[25] that his researches had revealed, in 1620, a Conveyance for a smallholding at Kirkdale-Banckes (sic). He reported, 'His (Nicholas Postgate's) mother is definitely identified (as Margaret) by the Conveyance of a farm or small-holding which she worked at Kirkdale-Banckes (sic) in 1620.' He does not suggest a locale for Kirkdale Banks, whilst Peacock states that Nicholas was born at Kirkdale House in the parish of Egton[26] and Margaret Urquhart's article categorically states, 'James Postgate, the father of Nicholas Postgate, lived at Kirkdale Banks, Egton.'[27] In those references to Kirkdale Banks, none mentions Egton Bridge.

The conveyance in question was some twenty years after the birth of Nicholas Postgate but before he went to Douai which suggests he lived there as a child when his mother was a widow. His father, James, also lived here[28] but he died in 1602 when Nicholas was a small child. It is therefore abundantly clear that Nicholas lived at Kirkdale Banks when very young and it was indeed the family home. But does that prove he was born there? Father Quinlan's terminology suggests Margaret Postgate owned it when she was a widow—he says she *worked* the smallholding or farm. She did not work *at* it for someone else—she worked that plot of land and that implies it belonged to her. This seems to be the first recorded link between Kirkdale Banks and the Postgates: in the 1604 Recusants Lists for Egton, a Mr and Mrs Smithson and a servant are also recorded as living at Kirkedale Bank (sic), and Margery White, wife of Robert, is also shown there.

My discovery of three dwellings on the 1636 map, all beside a track leading through Kirkdale Banks, suggests this was a hamlet containing those two families with a third house belonging to James and Margaret Postgate. I believe those houses have since been incorporated within West Banks, an existing farm near that site. That was a common practice and I have found no trace of the old houses.

I possess three copies of local Ordnance Survey maps dating from c.1843 into modern times, with scales of 1" to the mile, 2.5" to the mile and 6" to the mile but none records Kirkdale Banks at Egton Bridge or anywhere else. However, the copy of my 1636 map does identify that location—on a modern map it would span the area at MRs 780066 and 783066. In 1636, therefore, Kirkdale Banks was definitely at Egton, not Egton Bridge and its postal address is now Glaisdale, only some 300–400 yards from the house where I was born at Thorneywaite, Glaisdale (we left when I was a few months old).

This information leaves no doubt that the young Nicholas Postgate and other family members lived at Kirkdale Banks, Egton, but was Nicholas actually born there? Kirkdale Banks is not Kirkdale House and I think it is necessary to remember that the Recusants Lists do not name individual houses, merely the hamlets or villages in which they were located. Furthermore, there is no reference to Kirkdale House, Egton Bridge in the Recusants Lists, although both Kirkdale and Kirkdale Banks do feature in the Egton returns.

(e) Where or what was Kirkdale?

In North Yorkshire, there is a small valley known as Kirkdale and it is near Kirkbymoorside. It contains a very historic former Catholic church now known as Kirkdale Minster close to the historic Kirkdale Cave. But that Kirkdale is some fifteen miles away to the south of the moors.

It is not 'our' Kirkdale. Ours is another Kirkdale near Egton. The word 'kirk' features prominently in place-names around Yorkshire and into Scotland. Some North Yorkshire examples include Kirkby-in-Cleveland, Kirkby Knowle, Kirkbymoorside, Kirkham Priory and Oswaldkirk. There are others in Scotland and the North of England where *kirk* means the same thing—it is the local word for 'church'. Dale is the Yorkshire name for a valley, thus Kirkdale suggests a valley associated with a church.

Whether Egton *Bridge* at the time of Father Postgate's birth had a church is in doubt although there used to be a chapel on its bridge prior to 1400. The fate of the bridge is not known, although it was probably destroyed by flood water (which would also destroy the chapel). Such floods devastated a 14th century bridge two miles upriver at Glaisdale. The precise date of that particular flood is not known, except that the 14th century foundations of an early bridge at Glaisdale survived. In the 17th century, they were utilised in the construction of Beggar's Bridge built in 1619 by Tom Ferris. He was a former pirate and later Mayor of Hull, and his bridge spans the River Esk to this day near Glaisdale Railway Station. It was earlier known as Ferris Bridge or Ferry's Bridge but it appears on my 1636 map as Ferry Bridge. There is no record of a chapel there. There is no doubt that Nicholas Postgate both as a youngster and as a priest would have used that bridge.

However, because there was a chapel on Egton Bridge's bridge around 1400, we must ask whether any area of Egton Bridge could have become known as Kirkdale. It seems possible but unlikely and I have found no trace of 'Kirkdale' on maps relating to that village. As a matter of some interest, the 1604 *List of Roman Catholics in the County of York*[29] refers to the Bridgeholme Green area of Egton Bridge as Egton-Brigg-End whilst never referring to Kirkdale at Egton Bridge.

Egton Bridge has rarely been without a bridge. Details of earlier one are difficult to obtain but one was constructed there in 1758 — without a chapel. It was washed away in the floods of 1930 to be superseded by a temporary structure that survived for more than 60 years until 1993. That is when the present stone bridge was completed and it is said to be a copy of the 1758 structure.

However, St. Hilda's *original* Church at Egton is more than a mile away from Egton Bridge and it dates from the 13th century or possibly earlier. Precisely when Egton Bridge became the name of a community rather than merely a bridge is uncertain although it probably received that name during the 16th century.[30] The succession of bridges at this location (apparently without chapels) occurred because it was an important route to York and the south.

The area near Egton Bridge's bridge is known as Holm Wath. *Holm* means a stretch of land near a river or stream and *wath* is a ford across a river or stream. Both *holm* and *wath* feature regularly in local place names and in this case, the name of the local manor house, Bridgeholme Green—(once known as Brigham and home of the aristocratic Smith family)—indicates its presence near both a bridge and a holm. And even in my time at the local school, there used to be a wath nearby. Traces can still be seen. Not surprisingly the surrounding area is known as Bridge Holm whilst the word *green* suggests an open area of grass, probably accessible by the public.

But I have discovered another Bridge Holm in the former Egton Parish. It is at the foot of Church Dale and was known as Oak Bridge Holm, ie: land below The Grange at Glaisdale. It would be easy to confuse Bridge Holm at Egton with its namesake in Egton Bridge, especially as both are on the banks of the River Esk. But could this have led to a belief that Kirkdale, with Oak Bridge Holm at its foot, was in Egton Bridge, whereas it was really a small dale below Egton's old church?

In tracing the footsteps of Nicholas Postgate, we must remember that Egton was a village in its own right, with Egton Parish being both important and extensive because it included other small communities. It is about a mile uphill from Egton Bridge which is perhaps best described as a hamlet—certainly would be in the 17th century. Egton was a substantial community with a market, albeit small by modern standards. Its old church of St Hilda stood half-a-mile from Egton's village centre along Glaisdale Lane and in its heyday it would have been the focus for the villagers of Egton and most of that expansive parish. The present church on that site is not the original. It is Egton Mortuary Chapel built on the site of the former church of St Hilda in 1897 and making use of some original materials and stonework. The importance of that little church to the families who lived in the dale below (namely Kirk-dale) and on the moors nearby cannot be over-estimated. That was especially so in Nicholas Postgate's time and it was this valley full of Catholics that became known as a 'bishopric of papists'.

The parish of Egton, which was part of the wider parish of Lythe, included both Egton Bridge and Grosmont Priory as well as several hamlets spread over a wide area. Their names appear regularly on Egton Recusants Lists. They include (in a variety of spellings) Growmanhurst (Grosmont), Mirkebeck (Mirkside), Egton Bridge, Linderberhill (Limber Hill), Egton Wood (now Arncliffe Wood), Kirkedale, Kirkdale Banks, Westonby, Okebar Holme (Oak Bridge Holm), Shortwayte (Shortwaite), Egton Banks, West Banks, Horse Mire Head (then between Egton and Aislaby) and Leaserigg. (On yet another personal note, my great grandparents used to farm at Limber Hill and some of my ancestors are buried in the graveyard that lay beside the old Church of St Hilda at the head of Kirkdale).

Today, many of the above names apply to farmsteads rather than hamlets but in the past, a farmstead was of considerable size and accommodated several workers' families in cottages or within the farmhouse itself. Many such farms were known as hamlets, a hamlet being a community without a church and without a set of stocks.

Neither Church Dale nor Church Dale House appears on the Egton Recusants Lists. Quite simply, they were not known by those names at that time. They would be called Kirkdale and Kirkdale House or perhaps Kirk House as I shall describe later—but Kirk-dale House does not appear on those Recusants Lists either.

However, in 1599/1600, the probable year of Father Postgate's birth, Egton Parish was known, even at national level, as 'a bishopric of Papists with Grosmont Abbey as its head house'.[31] The village of Grosmont did not exist consequently 'Grosmont', in its variety of spellings, referred to the priory which was not an abbey.

So did that 'bishopric' refer to a concentration of papists in and around Egton Bridge? I think not—apart from the aristocratic Smiths, few recusants lived in Egton Bridge as the Recusants Lists confirm. Their greatest concentration was in the remote country-side around that old church at Egton. 133 recusants were listed there in 1614—an ideal breeding ground for a future martyr.

(f) Was Nicholas Postgate's 'Kirkdale House' really at Egton?

Egton's old church of St Hilda, heart of the former Catholic parish, is now a re-constructed Mortuary Chapel adjoining the present graveyard. Its Catholic history is confirmed by a papal indulgence granted in 1291 to penitents who visited the Church,[32] and on 6th June, 1349 it was dedicated by the Bishop of Damascus. It suffered dreadfully after the Reformation and during the infamous Edwardine Visitation. To prevent its use for Catholic services, its interior was ransacked, the altar smashed, precious statues and ornaments thrown out, woodwork handed to local people, and wall decorations white-washed to obliterate its Catholic origins. Later, its font was thrown down Kirk Cliff in front of the church but later recovered and installed in the new Anglican Church at either Egton or Goathland.

Such was the damage that the church was considered unsafe and eventually in 1876 it was ruthlessly demolished with items and stonework being removed for inclusion in Egton's new Anglican Church. A Pre-Reformation chalice and communion set disappeared and the bells were removed to Egton's new St Hilda's Church.[33] The present Mortuary Chapel occupies the site and the new St Hilda's Church at Egton was built in 1878, a mile or so away but very close to Father Postgate's Mass House.

Stretching to the west of that old cemetery lies a range of modest hills broadly known as Egton Banks. A steep but minor road called Bank Lane passes through. Between Egton Banks and the lane to Glaisdale there is a minor dale with streams cascading from the moors to join the River Esk opposite Glaisdale cricket field. Today it is called Church Dale and its main stream is Church Dale Beck which flows into the Esk. There are five farms (former hamlets) in this vicinity—Westonby, West Banks, Egton Banks, Thorn Hill Farm and Church Dale Farm. Together, the latter four once formed the hamlet of West Banks with Church Dale Farm formerly being known as Church Dale *House*. It bears that name on my Ordnance Survey map of Glaisdale Parish, first surveyed in 1849-53, and revised in both 1911 and 1930. Current Ordnance Survey maps show the building as Church Dale *Farm,* not 'house'. In Father Postgate's time, Westonby was a hamlet in its own right with one large house and smaller ones nearby. It was the home of the renowned Simpsons or Egton Players (see Chapter 2). One oddity here is that some of the farms also bear the names of a wider area—both Egton Banks and West Banks are names of farms as well as small ill-defined areas close to Kirkdale Banks.

Let us now consider the early Ordnance Survey officials who visited locations that would feature on their maps. To correctly identify a location they were frequently compelled to ask the people, especially in rural areas, for the local name of a particular place. Sometimes the replies would be in dialect which may not be suitable for a national map. This was especially the case in places such as Scotland, Wales and Cornwall but the local people did not like their local names being tampered with. Nonetheless, it meant that many names had to be converted into standard English.

So would surveyors researching the first Ordnance Survey maps have used the names of Church Dale House, Church Dale Beck or

Church Cliff at Egton also to avoid using 'Kirkdale' due to confusion with its namesake near Kirkbymoorside?

Bearing in mind that 'kirk' was often used for 'church' in this part of Yorkshire, it would not be pronounced in its Anglicised form. In the local dialect—which I spoke as a child—it was pronounced something like *Korruk* or a short guttural form of *cork* with a rolling of the 'r'. I am sure a nationally-aware surveyor would suggest that 'church' was a far better word for the forthcoming nationwide maps and the surveyors did have access to 'Name Books' that offered guidance with problematic names. Sadly, those books for England and Wales were destroyed in World War II.

However, my thoughts turned to the probability that, in the past, the people of Egton would probably have used local names for the locations in and around what is now Church Dale—Kirk Dale House, Kirk Dale Beck and Kirk Cliff due to the proximity of the old kirk adjoining the graveyard at the top of the hill. If this had been so, then puts a whole new complexion on that part of Egton.

As I continued my research, I felt that the vanished and forgotten Kirkdale Banks might have been very close to the area now called Church Dale, so could Church Dale House (Farm) in its old name of Kirk Dale House be the real birthplace of Nicholas Postgate? There is more evidence. At Egton, my 1843 OS map features St Hilda's old church at the head of Church Dale and to the south-west there is a substantial building called Church Dale House (not farm). Church Dale Beck flows down that dale to join the River Esk opposite what is now Glaisdale Cricket Field. The place where it joins the Esk is Oak Bridge Holm to which I referred earlier.

On a map of the North-East of Yorkshire in *'The Yorkshire Coast and the Cleveland Hills and Dales'* by John Leyland (1892) two locations at Egton are shown—Westonby House and Oak Bridge Holm. That indicates the significance of both, for each contained a range of unidentified buildings. I repeat an earlier query—could there have been some past confusion between Bridge Holm in Egton Bridge and Oak Bridge Holm in Church Dale (Kirkdale) at Egton? If Church Dale had been known as Kirkdale in the 17th century, it is very likely a simple error could have occurred to be perpetuated down the years in connection with Father Postgate's birthplace. And indeed, we cannot ignore the fact that the name of Egton derives from oak, the old village name, Egetune, meaning 'a town of oaks'. So might Oak Bridge Holm have once been called Egton Bridge Holm?

But does the existence of two 'bridge holms' close to the River Esk and little over a mile apart, support the theory that the birthplace of Father Postgate was the original Church Dale House in Church Dale at Egton, almost two miles from its supposed site? If the place now called Church Dale Farm was the martyr's birthplace, it would probably not be the house that stands there today.

There may have been an earlier one of that name that has been incorporated within the present farmhouse or its outbuildings. However, an index of listed buildings suggests those farm-buildings date from the 19th century while Church Dale House (Farm), itself a Grade II listed building, probably dates from the 18th century.

Its near neighbour, Egton Banks Farm, also dates from the 18th century but it is known there was an earlier house on the latter site because it features in the Recusants Lists of 1614 as does the nearby West Banks Farm. The appearance of these names in the Recusants Lists coupled with the information on the 1636 map tells us there were earlier houses on those sites, doubtless now incorporated within more recent structures. And surely if recusants, including the Postgates, lived at the premises now known as Church Dale Farm, or elsewhere in Church Dale at unnamed properties, those addresses would have appeared in the Recusants Lists? But they don't, either as Church Dale House or Kirk Dale House.

So could there have been a Kirkdale House on a nearby site in that dale during the 17th century? I think it is possible. Higher up the dale between Egton Banks and Westonby there was a patch of land known as Kirkdale Intake with a dwelling upon it. Intakes (areas of land recovered from the moor) were named either after the person who enclosed it or the property to which it was attached. Limber Intake was not far from Limber Hill Farm whilst White Intake was probably the work of the local White family (A family called White lived at Kirkdale Banks—see above in this chapter).

So if Kirkdale Intake had a dwelling upon it, is it feasible it could be known as Kirkdale House? If so, there is no sign of it today but a footpath runs past the old site. It is quite possible it degenerated into a pile of unwanted stones, little more than a cattle shed!

My map that covers an area of *The Lordship of Egton in the County of York, in 1636* does not name features such as streams, houses or farms but does highlight fields and intakes by name whilst indicating dwellings or buildings by the use of small black squares or oblong marks. On the site of the current Church Dale Farm it shows either Beacon Hill or Beacon Hall plus buildings. That is not there now.

So maybe there was then no Kirkdale House or Church Dale House at that location? That would be all the more reason for believing there was once a Kirkdale House at Kirkdale Intake higher up the dale. Kirkdale and Kirkdale Banks are both named in the Recusants Lists but not the name of Postgate at Kirkdale House.

Of immense interest, therefore, is that whilst this old map shows the early Egton Church as 'Church', it lists the fields and intakes around it with a prefix of Kirk. They are Kirk Fields, Kirke Field (twice), Low Kirk Intake, Kirk Cliff—and Kirkdale Intake. Significantly, my modern OS map shows 'Church Cliff' whereas my 1636 map identifies it as Kirk Cliff—at precisely the same location. All this is strong circumstantial evidence that the entire Church Dale was at that time known as Kirk Dale. If that was so, then today's Church Dale Beck would have been Kirkdale Beck and Church Dale House (Farm) would have been Kirkdale House or Kirkdale Farm. But there is yet more evidence because this map actually shows an area called Kirkdale Banks which is absent from all my more recent maps. So Kirkdale Banks, the home of both James and Margaret Postgate when James died in 1602 (when Nicholas was very young) can be placed close to the present Stonegate Beck where it joins the River Esk near Rake Farm, Glaisdale (see map on p. 4).

It is at least two miles from Egton Bridge and further by road or footpath. I have already provided its modern map reference and referred to the three un-named buildings upon it during the lifetime of Nicholas Postgate, all close to a track or path.

At that time, it is possible that such houses would not be individually named. They would be identified as merely being situated at Kirkdale Banks plus the name of the occupants.

On a completely different level, there is a piece of local folklore that uses the name *kirk*. An evil ghostly creature was said to haunt the area around Egton's old church—Kirk Dale in other words—and its name was *kirk-grim*. Its appearance heralded death to anyone who looked upon it. That was long, long ago!

So was Nicholas Postgate born at Kirkdale Banks in a house that no longer exists but which might have been incorporated within the modern West Banks? Or was he born on the site of the house at the edge of Kirkdale Intake? Or could it have been a cottage on the site now known as Church Dale Farm? Or was it Kirkdale House in Egton Bridge? The Douai Diary entry published after his death records his place of birth as Kirkdale House in the parish of Egton.[34] However, the postal address of Church Dale Farm and its neighbouring properties is now Glaisdale and Church Dale Farm is a tenanted working farm owned by Mulgrave Estate. Coincidentally, it was the Dowager Marchioness of Normanby from Mulgrave Castle and Estate who donated to St Hedda's Church at Egton Bridge in July 2011 the stained glass window of Father Postgate that appears on the cover of this book.

However, despite strong evidence that James Postgate lived at Kirkdale Banks until he died in 1602 when Nicholas was a child, and that his mother inherited the house, there is nothing to prove that he or his siblings were born either there or at Kirkdale House. So where was Nicholas born? Could it have been that un-named family home at Kirkdale Banks? On the balance of probability, he was surely born there but lack of absolute proof means it is another mystery in the life of this martyr.

In the next chapter we follow the life of the teenage Nicholas Postgate.

Notes

[1]   Dom Bede Camm, *Forgotten Shrines* (Leominster: Gracewing, 2004), p. 281.

[2]   See *A List of the Roman Catholics in the County of York* (1604). Transcribed in 1872 from the original MS in the Bodleian Library, Oxford by Edward Peacock, FSA (1872).

[3]   Father David Quinlan, 'The Father Postgate Story' in *Whitby Gazette* (17 February 1967).

[4]   Monica P. Ventress, *A Little About Littlebeck* (2009), p. 2.

[5]   Map reproduced courtesy of North Yorkshire County Record Office, Refs: ZW(M) 1/5: MIC 1293.

[6]   Margaret Urquhart, 'Was Christopher Simpson a Jesuit?' in *The Journal of the Viola da Gamba Society* 21(1992).

[7]   *Ibid.*

[8]   Elizabeth Hamilton, *The Priest of the Moors* (London: DLT, 1980), p. 13.

[9]   Father William Storey, *Ven. Nicholas Postgate* (London: Catholic Truth Society: 1928), p. 2.

10   See H. Foley, SJ, *Records of the English Province*, vol.V, p. 757.
11   Margaret Urquhart, 'Was Christopher Simpson a Jesuit?' in *The Journal of the Viola da Gamba Society* 21(1992).
12   *A List of the Roman Catholics in the County of York* (1604).
13   Storey, *Ven. Nicholas Postgate*, p. 2.
14   Hamilton, *The Priest of the Moors*, p. 12.
15   Storey, *Ven. Nicholas Postgate*, p. 2.
16   *Ibid.*
17   Urquhart, 'Was Christopher Simpson a Jesuit?'
18   Patricia Blackburn, *A short account of the missionary priests who served Ugthorpe and Egton Bridge during the Penal Days* (Hearts of Oak: 2004).
19   Camm, *Forgotten Shrines*, p. 281.
20   Storey, *Ven. Nicholas Postgate*, p. 2.
21   *Ibid.*
22   Hamilton, *The Priest of the Moors*, p. 12.
23   Storey, *Ven. Nicholas Postgate*, p. 2.
24   Map Reference: ZW(M) 1/5; MIC 1293 (2207/152–8 and 2207/122).
25   Quinlan, 'The Father Postgate Story'.
26   *A List of the Roman Catholics in the County of York* (1604).
27   Urquhart, 'Was Christopher Simpson a Jesuit?'
28   *Ibid.*
29   *A List of the Roman Catholics in the County of York* (1604).
30   J. L. O'Connor, *Hearts of Oak* (website of the Blackburn Kitching ancestry).
31   *Ibid.*
32   See British History Online (www.british-history.ac.uk), Parishes, Egton.
33   Blackburn, *A short account of the missionary priests who served Ugthorpe and Egton Bridge during the Penal Days*.
34   The Doway Diary and Other Monuments (Leeds University Library).

CHAPTER 2

Growing Up

VERY LITTLE IS known about the childhood and youthful years of Nicholas Postgate. Growing up in a remote rural area of the North Riding of Yorkshire, now known as North Yorkshire due to the 1974 boundary changes, he could enjoy a natural playground in the surrounding countryside. He would have made his own entertainment and perhaps combined such activity with boyish exploration of the hilly, wooded locality in which he lived. His home area lay below the loftier heather-covered reaches of the moors and close to the banks of the River Esk.

It was an essentially rural area with most people being farmers, landowners or agricultural workers and so he would have acquired a deep understanding of the countryside and its people. Almost as soon as he could walk he would be expected to help around the farmstead or small-holding, caring for the livestock, feeding the poultry and geese, collecting their eggs, milking the cows, helping with the harvest of hay or corn and acting as a general labourer, always under his parents' guidance. His acquired skills would be particularly important due to the widowhood of his mother when aged only 23. With a young family and a busy smallholding/farm, she would need all the help that was available.

Even though young Nicholas would have been working from a very tender age, there would be some time to enjoy unfettered access to the woods, rivers, becks and moors surrounding Egton and the neighbouring district. Perhaps with his brothers or friends, he would explore Limber Wood and Arncliffe Wood which there

there in his time between Egton, Egton Bridge and Glaisdale.[1]
Arncliffe Wood—then known as Egton Wood—contained the
reputed secret cave of Robin Hood and so that hiding place was
always sought by inquisitive lads — but I never found it!

Alternatively, he could range across the wild moors high above
Egton, Lealholm and Glaisdale to the call of the curlew and the
grouse. The high moors were known as Blackamoor, the name
deriving from its central peak called Blakey, now site of the Lion
Inn dating from the fifteenth century. The stark treeless heights are
beautiful during the spring, summer and autumn, but can be deadly
in winter. Many travellers in former times lost their way and
perished in deep snow and ferocious weather; there are tales of
isolated communities being cut off for weeks or even months.
During the autumn, the moorland would be blessed by a deep
carpet of purple heather known as ling, vital for the livelihood of
the red grouse.

Today, Blackamoor is surrounded by the boundaries of the
North York Moors National Park. The western areas are grouped
into The Cleveland Hills whilst easterly moors bear their own
names, eg Egton High Moor, Glaisdale Moor, Goathland Moor
and others. The area of the North York Moors National Park is 553
square miles (1,432 square kilometres) and it lies many miles from
the Yorkshire Dales National Park. The North York Moors are
quite separate from the Yorkshire Dales.

The North York Moors are encircled by market towns, the coast
and seaside resorts, including Robin Hood's Bay, Whitby, Sandsend, Saltburn-by-the-Sea, Redcar, Guisborough, Stokesley, Thirsk,
Helmsley, Pickering and Scarborough. These towns, and the inland
heights within the boundaries they create, contain some of the most
interesting and beautiful landscape in England. It was here that the
adult Father Nicholas Postgate undertook his astonishing ministry
of the moors, perhaps relying on the experiences of his adventurous

childhood to guide him around this countryside which at times could be both charming and treacherous.

In his time, travel was mainly on foot. People did not walk for recreational purposes—they walked out of necessity.

Only the wealthy and perhaps some hill-farmers might afford a horse with or without a cart and so the moors and dales were criss-crossed with a network of footpaths and lanes. Paths called trods were surfaced with slabs of sandstone worn down by constant foot-traffic, some having survived since the 13th century or earlier. In Father Postgate's youth, one such trod stretched from the coast at Sandyford near Whitby via Dunsley and Skelder Plantation to cross the moors into Egton and thence into Egton Bridge. Another led from the coast at Kettleness, through East Barnby and eventually into Egton Bridge.

During Father Postgate's childhood, it is highly likely that priests secretly entered the country from overseas and made use of these trods, and that there would be several safe-houses along their routes and at their conclusion. Grosmont Priory, even in its semi-ruined state, was one of them and Mulgrave Castle another. Sandyford, a seaside village in Father Postgate's time, is now called Sandsend and it was there or nearby that most of the incoming priests came ashore. However, those trods were used by a variety of travellers ranging from monks to pedlars via pilgrims, wandering minstrels and local merchants with their trains of pack horses. Other users included rogues, vagabonds and robbers—and missionary priests.

One trod is reputed to have led from Whitby Abbey along the banks of the Esk to Glaisdale, and then continued over the lofty moors into Rosedale where a priory existed. Some lengths have survived—a stretch in Glaisdale dale is an example. Such a route would probably have continued beyond Rosedale Priory to Rievaulx Abbey with pilgrims and monks using it regularly. In Glaisdale Dale, to cater for travellers, there was a halt known as The Pilgrims'

Inn. It is now known as Postgate Farm and until recently was a bed-and-breakfast establishment. This farmhouse has followed an ancient tradition of always being open to guests.

As I pen these notes, its future is uncertain because it is for sale due to the owners' retirement. Even when I was a child, that route was known as Monks' Trod and one surviving stretch of another trod can be seen in Arncliffe Wood between Glaisdale and Egton Bridge. It is intriguing to think they would be there in Father Postgate's time, and that he would have used them.

Lonely stone crosses sometimes marked those routes, proving to be important guides and indicators when the deep snows covered the landscape; in some cases, Holy Mass was celebrated beside those crosses as people from remote communities gathered to greet a travelling priest. Most villages boasted tiny chapels, once part of a local abbey or priory and often situated on a bridge, but in Father Postgate's youth they were neglected and ruinous. Protestant 'reformers' had ransacked and plundered them. They had also destroyed everything in the parish churches that might be used in 'Papist' ceremonies and afterwards local people removed the stones to construct their own buildings.

For the adolescent Nicholas Postgate, however, there was an important local centre for his entertainment and probably his education. It is perhaps the proximity of this place, and the use to which it was put, that enabled him in later years to secure a prestigious Doctor of Divinity degree at the English College in Douai. But he would have experienced no such thoughts in his young head as he first walked from Egton to the partial ruins of Grosmont Priory. Although situated within the parish of Egton, the ruins were some two miles from Kirkdale's St Hilda's Church. There was no village of Grosmont at that time although scattered farms and cottages occupied lonely sites on the surrounding moors and hillsides. Fortunately, total ruination of Grosmont Priory by

Henry VIII's commissioners was far from complete and the former buildings remained habitable for many years as a working farm.

At its foundation, it was known as an alien cell of the Abbey of Grandimont of Normandy in France and was created a priory by Johanna, the daughter of William Fossard. Johanna was the wife of Robert de Torneham. It is believed her priory was established in the thirteenth century during the reign of King John of England (1167–1216). He was known for his tyranny, a matter that prompted the barons to force him to sign the Magna Carta. However, Richard II (1367–1400) dissolved all the alien priories in England and so the premises were sold to John Hewitt, sometimes known as John Sergeant. Under his ownership, the premises continued to function as a priory although it was very small with only four monks. It was then dissolved for a second time, on this occasion by King Henry VIII in 1535, when it was valued at £12.2s.8d. (£12.14p). Nonetheless, this tiny ruined priory, with its half-complete inhabited buildings, was destined to play a vital role in the survival of the Catholic faith, especially in Yorkshire.

The wealthy Cholmley family of Whitby bought the abbey lands of both Whitby and Grosmont, and being a determined Catholic and recusant family, set about putting their purchases to good and profitable use. Grosmont Priory, sometimes known as Growmondhurst, was rented to a farmer called John Hodgson, himself a devout Catholic. Ably assisted by the powerful Cholmley family, whose relations included the Earl of Northumberland, the Earl of Cumberland, the noted Scropes of Bolton Castle, the Constables of the East Riding and a host of other local gentry and landowners, this tiny former priory was developed into what amounted to a staging post for priests. It accommodated those who arrived in secret on the North-East coast before embarking upon their mission further inland. The Cholmley's mansion adjoining the ruined Abbey at

Whitby was also used to accommodate incoming missionary priests who arrived at or near Whitby. It is now open to the public.

With highly supportive Catholic neighbours all around the Egton area, priests could arrive on the Yorkshire coast and safely travel inland to find shelter and food in a various houses. All safe-houses were marked with the sign of the Five Wounds of Christ—five tiny scratches were made on the stone work in the form of an X and this told the newcomer that it was safe, and that board and bed was always available. To qualify as a safe-house, it must have at least two doors to allow an escape route for the priest if cornered. Bridgeholme Green at Egton Bridge, the manor of the Smith family, was a safe-house and it had seven doors with food and lodgings always freely available. Accommodating these incoming missionary priests became a highly developed and secretive business that evaded the Protestant authorities. The incoming priests travelled in disguise, often in pairs, pretending to be a merchant and his assistant or adopting some other dual role. Grosmont Priory, described as a remote farmhouse and considered of little interest to the authorities, suddenly found itself a focus for the shelter, accommodation and training of incoming priests in open defiance of the State authorities. It is not surprising that one Government spy described Grosmont Priory as '*the head house of a papist bishopric*'.[2] Certainly it attracted the attention of the Protestant authorities but the tenant farmer, John Hodgson, managed to evade many of their raids on his home, even though he once found himself before the Court of High Commissioners in York with a possible charge of treason hanging over him. Fortunately, no action was taken, probably due to lack of evidence and he continued to admit priests to his home. Not only did he receive priests who arrived on the Yorkshire coastline, he also admitted those who came ashore secretly as far north as South Shields on the Durham coast.

Whilst at their priests' training college at Douai or other overseas colleges, the young priests were encouraged to take part as actors in plays or interludes and what were known as 'skits'. This was a valuable part of their recreation but it also taught them to speak in public and to face an audience that might sometimes be critical. When they came ashore in England, therefore, and gathered in secret places like Grosmont Priory, they entertained themselves —and the local people—with their plays, jokes, interludes, music and skits. We might refer to skits as short comedy sketches or parodies. Making use of them to poke fun at the Church of England, however, was made illegal by Parliament.

Performances on stage or perhaps out-of-doors were popular throughout England by groups known as strolling players and as the young Nicholas Postgate was growing up, playwrights called William Shakespeare and Ben Jonson had already made names for themselves. It has long been claimed that Shakespeare's plays contained hidden Catholic messages—his parents were recusants, his sister was a Catholic and it is thought he spent some of his adolescent years at a secret Catholic address in Lancashire. This was a period known as Shakespeare's lost years between 1585 and 1592. At that time, a William Shakeshafte worked as a page or servant at Houghton Tower in Lancashire, this being a safe house for priests complete with a hiding place. It was also home of the Houghton family who were involved in the establishment of Douai as a training college for English Catholic priests. If the name Shakeshafte casts doubt on the authenticity of this story, then it is interesting to note that Shakespeare's grandfather called himself Shakspere, Shakstaff and Shakeschafte.

There can be little doubt that some of Shakespeare's plays were performed at Grosmont Priory —and that his work influenced the young Nicholas Postgate but there was also a group of strolling players based in Egton.

They were known as The Simpsons and the family was then based at Westonby, a hamlet in Egton parish near Kirkdale (now Church Dale). It is currently a farmhouse. The Simpsons performed in large country houses, various halls and even in the open air at venues around the West, East and North Ridings of Yorkshire. Undoubtedly, the young Nicholas Postgate would be fully aware of the role offered by the busy former priory, particularly its open defiance of the authorities within a pervading air of secrecy and intrigue. So when the opportunity arose for him to join the Simpsons, he accepted.

But here arises another of those mysteries surrounding the young Nicholas Postgate—was this young strolling player the future martyr of the moors, or was he another Nicholas Postgate? Many researchers have concluded there was no other man or youth of that name within that locality, and yet Father David Quinlan discovered another. He was a Nicholas Postgate who lived at Sleights but was a few years older than the Nicholas of Kirkdale House. However, accounts of the activities of the Simpsons state that all the group's members came from Egton (namely Egton Parish) which tends to rule out his Sleights name-sake. My own opinion is that, on the balance of probabilities, the Nicholas Postgate who became that strolling player was indeed our martyr. My reasons are revealed in the subsequent activities of Father Postgate and the youthful influences that moulded his opinions.

So how did this young lad from Egton come to be a member of a renowned or perhaps notorious group of strolling players known as the Simpsons' Players or the Egton Interlude Players? They were regarded as vagrants and liable to prosecution but that was effective only when they performed beyond the boundaries of their own parish—and the Simpsons invariably chose to perform far away from Egton parish boundaries.

All the players came from within Egton parish boundaries and they actually performed Shakespeare's *King Lear* on the first recorded occasion it was staged outside London. *King Lear*, although presented on the London stage, was first printed in 1608 and it was performed by the Egton players only one year later in 1609. The part of Lear was played by Christopher Simpson, Cordelia by Thomas Pant and the Fool by William Harrison. At that time, there were no female actors, female parts being played by youths or men. There were other Shakespearian influences upon their work and the players were able to obtain most of the newly printed plays from London. Attending plays was a very fashionable past-time. Both Shakespeare and Ben Jonson were writing and performing highly popular works at that time and they won a massive following throughout the country.

The Simpsons won their plaudits because they poked fun at, and created parodies of, the Church of England through skits, songs, music, plays and interludes. All were Catholic recusants living in the Egton area which, in the *Calendar of State Papers Domestic 1598-1601* had been declared *A bishopric of Papists*. This was an area to the west of Egton village which included Egton Banks, West Banks, Kirkdale Banks and Westonby. These locations appeared frequently in recusant returns over many years (see Chapter 1).

In fact, the Catholics of Egton and district were in open contempt of the harsh anti-Catholic laws and their activities had attracted the attention of Parliament. Thus the Catholics of Egton parish were of national renown and they were a proverbial thorn in the flesh of the Protestant authorities. No doubt the activities of the highly popular Simpson Players helped to keep the faith alive on the moors whilst giving local people a boost of confidence along with a wonderful sense of freedom to express concern about their persecuted faith.

The leader was Christopher Simpson (1590–1647). He lived in the hamlet of Westonby, very close to West Banks, Egton Banks and Kirkdale Banks. His activities had led to the Lord Chief Justice declaring him a rogue in 1614, then later, he and his family went to live at Hunt House, Goathland. According to Margaret Urquhart's article 'Was Christopher Simpson a Jesuit?', Christopher Simpson had a son also called Christopher who lived at Hunt House, and who became a nationally acclaimed musician and composer.[3] In her article she raises the possibility that this Christopher became a Jesuit priest who was educated overseas at St Omer, a town close to the coast of North-East France. From there, he returned to the English Mission at Durham. There is no space in this book to develop that fascinating story.

To continue with the Egton players, a Robert Simpson who was either Christopher's brother or his uncle lived at Staithes.[4] He married Alice Postgate but her relationship to Nicholas is not known. Other members of the troupe were John Simpson, Richard Simpson, Edward Whitfield, James Button, Edward Consett, Francis Danby, George Ellerby, William Featherstone, Robert Harbutt (sometimes known as Cordiner), William Harrison, George Hodgson, Richard Knaggs, John Lee, Robert Lounde, Edward Millington, Thomas Pant, James Pickering, Nicholas Postgate and George White. They did not always perform together—some took part in only a few tours whilst performances sometimes required a small cast. Eventually, some cast members lived outside Egton parish, probably due to marriage or work.

In carrying out their illegal tours, the players were sponsored, their main supporter being Richard Cholmley, son of Sir Henry Cholmley, Lord of the Manor at Whitby with important links to other noble families. His grandmother, for example, was the eldest daughter of the first Earl of Cumberland.

Richard was also related to the powerful Scrope family of Castle Bolton in Wensleydale, all strong, ardent Catholics.

It was due to the influence of the Cholmley family that the Simpsons were able to secure early editions of Shakespeare's plays. In addition to Cholmley's support and sponsorship, the players received valuable assistance from other people during their tours. Wherever they performed, they required food, rest and accommodation. A fine example is evident in their tour that began on 29th December 1614/15 and ended on 18th February, 1615/16—the one that resulted in Nicholas Postgate being fined.[5]

Supporters at all the venues on that tour were each fined ten shillings, the venues being Buttercrambe, New Malton, Hovingham, Gilling, Whenby, Brandsby, Easingwold, Thirsk, Kirby Wiske, Ainderby Steeple, South Otterington, Thornton-le-Moor, Burneston, Middleham, Masham, Bolton-on-Swale, Bedale, Aldborough, Brompton, Osmotherley, Swainby, Great Ayton, Marton, Wilton, Marske, Skelton, Danby, Egton Bridge, Hutton Buscel and East Ayton near Scarborough. Many of their supporters, but not all, were Catholics. Indeed, some belonged to the Church of England but they supported these popular and, at times, libellous plays and jests.

However, as a consequence of that tour, the law caught up with Nicholas Postgate. As a member of the performers known as The Simpsons from Egton, he was charged with vagrancy and appeared at Helmsley Quarter Sessions on 9th January 1615/16 where he was fined ten shillings (50p)—a huge amount when a schoolmaster's salary was around £4 per annum. It is this fine that casts some doubt upon whether this Nicholas was our martyr. Court records showed him to be a labourer from Egton aged 13 at the time of the offence but it is worthy of record that some court hearings were three years after the offence.[6]

However, there does not appear to have been such a delay in this case. By my reckoning, if Nicholas was born in, say 1600, he could have been fifteen at the time of the offence, particularly if he took part in early performances (not every actor took part in every performance). In chapter 2 I mentioned difficulties in establishing precise dates but the truth is we do not know exactly when Father Postgate was born.

Even at his death, he is variously shown as being aged between 79 and 82 or 83. I believe those doubts lean towards the culprit being the future Father Postgate. Another clue maybe that the Nicholas Postgate who was prosecuted described himself as a labourer from Egton—as indeed he would be if he worked on his mother's smallholding. However, I believe that his strong faith, love of music and associated activities indicate that he was indeed that culprit.

The continuing defiance by all recusants in the Egton area became an obsession for one man sent by the Government to arrest them and force them to attend Church of England services. He was Sir Thomas Posthumous Hoby, his middle name arising because he was born after the death of his father. A magistrate, he lived at Hackness near Scarborough but had powerful links with some of the country's top politicians—his mother, for example, was the sister-in-law of Lord Burghley (William Cecil), one of Queen Elizabeth I's most trusted ministers. Hoby was also cousin of Sir Robert Cecil, the chief minister to James I and later Lord Salisbury. He was a fervent Puritan with an intense dislike of Catholics, but the Yorkshire gentry with whom he tried to mix socially regarded him as both a foreigner and interloper. They poked fun at him and his behaviour, resulting in a long running feud between Sir Richard Cholmley and Sir Thomas Hoby. Sir Thomas' wife, Lady Margaret Hoby, was also something of a socialite who seemed to enjoy being driven around in a smart coach to visit friends at places like Nunnington Hall and Snape Castle.

Nonetheless she was also very considerate to the poor and needy, and worked hard in her own home at Hackness.[7] She appears to have enjoyed more social success than her husband, but they lived together in happiness for 37 years at Hackness. Lady Hoby died in 1633 and there is a memorial to her in the ancient church at Hackness.

There is no doubt that Sir Richard Cholmley encouraged the Simpsons to poke fun at the Puritianical Sir Thomas and the entire English establishment. Indeed it is said that Shakespeare's puritanical clown and misery Malvolio was based on Sir Thomas Hoby. This arose after Sir Thomas was involved in a renowned court case against his Yorkshire neighbours in 1600. He sued them because it was alleged they had come completely uninvited to his home at Hackness where they had drunk heavily, played cards and poked fun at his religion and Puritanical beliefs. There was even an allegation they had threatened to rape Lady Margaret Hoby. Sir Thomas won his case and was awarded damages.

However, his lack of success, both socially and authoritatively made Sir Thomas more determined to force the recusants of Egton to conform to the Church of England, but despite his efforts he had very little success.

All this fuss, of course, increased the notoriety of the Egton area. It was seen as an increasingly powerful recusant district. It was due to Hoby's connections and friends in high places in London that the Catholics of Egton became very well known to Parliament and to important advisers and ministers of the sovereign. Indeed, that national notoriety was to continue for many years. But with each lack of success, the Protestant authorities became even more determined to eradicate Catholicism from that moorland area, but always failed.

There can be no doubt that these high-level politics were observed by the youthful Nicholas Postgate through his association with the Simpsons and his visits to Grosmont Priory. If, therefore, one asks how a small community like Egton managed to produce and sustain such a powerful and skilled band of strolling players drawn from ordinary men within their midst, the answer might lie at the other side of the German Ocean at the English College in Douai.

As a form of entertainment, the trainee priests would stage plays and musical interludes, and it is known that many, on returning to England after ordination, spent time at Grosmont Priory. It is very likely the young Nicholas Postgate also attended Mass there and probably visited the old priory for entertainment and parties, perhaps alone or with his mother and members of his family.

Furthermore, it is possible that the Simpsons learned a lot of their techniques and skills through being coached by priests who arrived from Douai and stayed awhile in Grosmont before heading off to their missions. In realising the players' links with Shakespeare, one can understand the likely effect his work might have had upon the young Nicholas Postgate.

Later in chapters 6 and 7, there are accounts of him secretly working as a priest on Blackamoor where he would spread sheets on hedgerows to announce the location of Mass, and he also planted daffodils to signify the baptism of a child or a convert to Catholicism. Most certainly he planted small wild daffodils around his modest home at Ugthorpe. This tiny place was originally known as *Mr Postgate's*, only later being called The Hermitage—a misnomer because he was never a hermit.

In seeking secret emblems or signs to signify his belief in the resurrection of Catholicism despite the efforts of the English State, could the maturing Nicholas Postgate have recalled these words from Shakespeare in The Winter's Tale?

When daffodils begin to peer,
With heigh! The doxy, over the dale,

Why, then comes in the sweet o' the year;
For the red blood reigns in the winter's pale.
The white sheets bleaching on the hedge,
With heigh! The sweet birds, O how they sing,
Doth set my pugging tooth on edge
For a quart of ale is a dish for a king.

It is highly likely that Nicholas Postgate's association with the Simpsons left an indelible mark upon his young mind. This would manifest itself both when he attended any of their plays, interludes and skits and certainly when he joined the players on tour. Those memories would be imprinted on his mind as when he left Egton to train for the priesthood.

Perhaps the strongest memory resulted from the players wanting to stress their Catholicity and remind their audiences about Catholic history in England. To make a huge impact, they flourished a yellow cross in the form of an X, usually embroidered upon a banner or flag. This was the abbreviated form of the Five Wounds of Christ, an emblem used down the centuries as a sign of Catholicism being a united religion throughout the world. It was also a symbol of resistance to those who would attempt to destroy the faith. In the newly Protestant England, this could be seen as a highly provocative symbol in whatever form it was displayed. It had been used much earlier, however. Crusaders from European countries displayed the Five Wounds of Christ during their sorties against the Muslims (1096–1291). It was done to assert their Christianity whilst later in England (1536–7) it was carried on a banner by members of the ill-fated Pilgrimage of Grace as a protest against Henry VIII's suppression of the monasteries.

*Figure 1: Banner of the Five Wounds of Christ carried during the
Pilgrimage of Grace, 1536*[8]

At the time of Father Postgate, both during his childhood and
as an adult, it appeared both as a rallying emblem, a symbol of
resistance to a new and oppressive authority and a symbolic sign
of re-assurance for Catholics during the Penal Times. In all Catholic
churches, the altar stone also bore the image in the form of five
small X-marks carved upon the stone, one in each corner and one
in the centre to produce a larger X image.

The symbol was also carved on the portable altar stones carried
by missionary priests and an abbreviated form was scratched on
the doorways of safe-houses so that travelling priests knew they
could safely enter and remain there.

The potency of the Five Wounds of Christ in its X-form, in
whatever style that X was presented, can be compared with waving
a national flag or even a scarf in the colours of a modern football

team. In other words, the sight of the X, often coloured yellow, often provoked a reaction. It was used by the Simpsons during their performances; in one of their plays called *Saint Christopher* they used '*a great yallowe cross*'[9] and it also appeared in a specially adapted Catholic version of that play that touched upon the differences between Protestantism and Catholicism.

It emphasised the differences in a scene that depicted '*him that plaid the English minister and him that plaid the Popish priest.*' The actor portraying the Anglican minister argued for his religion on the basis of the Bible but the actor-priest countered by saying 'that was not enough and held up the yellow cross.'[10]

There can be little doubt that the young Nicholas Postgate regularly witnessed other examples of the X-symbol in its highly significant role. Even if he was not the Nicholas Postgate who had joined the Simpsons, he would still be aware of their activities and their use of powerful symbols in their plays. They were performed over a wide area with their coded messages, songs and carols, often with a subversive element. Examples of those sung and performed throughout England included *A New Dial* or *The Twelve Days of Christmas*. Another was altered in the aftermath of the Reformation, probably in 1625, and sung by Catholics as a rallying cry. It remains a well-known carol and is entitled '*Green Grow the Rushes Oh*'. Each verse relates in some oblique way to religion, ranging from God (*I'll sing you one, Oh*) via four for the gospel makers, ten for the commandments and twelve for the apostles.

The other numbers might not be so easy to understand but verse five is as follows:

I'll sing you five, oh,
Green grow the rushes, oh,
What is your five, oh?
Five for the symbols at your door,
Four for the gospel makers etc…

This is a reminder that the *'five symbols at your door'* appeared on safe houses where travelling priests could obtain rest and refreshment. The Five Wounds of Christ were those suffered during His crucifixion, but also the wound caused by the spear that pierced His side to determine whether He was alive or dead on the cross. In some portrayals of that image, His hands and feet are spread-eagled with His heart in the centre, whilst other images comprise only the shaft of the spear crossed with the shaft of the stick that carried the sponge of vinegar to His lips during His final moments. In all cases, there is a clear image of the X-mark.

Following the appearance of the young Nicholas Postgate at Helmsley Quarter Sessions on 9th January 1615/16 as a result of his participation in that tour of the Egton Players, we know nothing more of his life until he decided to become a priest and undertake the necessary training overseas at the English College in Douai, then in Flanders but now a town in northern France. Many years later, that would open him to a charge of high treason and another court appearance.

Notes

[1]   See British History Online (www.british-history.ac.uk), Parishes, Egton.

[2]   G. W. Boddy, 'Catholic Missioners at Grosmont Priory' in *North Yorkshire County Record Office Journal* 10(1976).

[3]   Margaret Urquhart, 'Was Christopher Simpson a Jesuit?' in Journal of the Viola da Gamba Society 21(1992), pp. 3–26.

[4]   G. W. Boddy, 'Catholic Missioners at Grosmont Priory' in *North Yorkshire County Record Office Journal* 10(1976).

[5]   A Robert Simpson, aged only seven, was also fined in 1616.

[6]   G. W. Boddy, 'Players of Interludes in North Yorkshire in the early seventeenth century' in *North Yorkshire County Record Office Journal* 3(1976).

7   John Rushton, *Yorkshire in the Reign of Elizabeth I* (Blackthorn Press: 2008).

8   This banner was created in embroidered textile by the English School (sixteenth century). This image is reproduced by kind permission of The Baroness Herries through the auspices of His Grace, The Duke of Norfolk, and the Bridgeman Art Library of London.

9   Boddy, 'Players of Interludes in North Yorkshire in the early seventeenth century'

10   *Ibid.*

CHAPTER 3

Douai

T HE NAME *DOUAI* features strongly in the history of the Penal Times in this country. There is absolutely no doubt that the establishment of the English College at Douai with its powerful teaching, dedicated staff and extremely brave newly-ordained priests, prevented the extinction of Catholicism in England and elsewhere. So where is Douai?

It is the name of a French town but usually we refer to the English College by that shortened and simple name of 'Douai.' What we really mean is The English College which was one of the colleges at the University of Douai. In Father Postgate's time as a student—the early seventeenth century—the town and its sur-rounds belonged to the Spanish Netherlands and Douai is situated on the River Scarpe not far from the present border with Belgium. It is about 50 km south of Lille. It has a population of around 43,000 and its main industries are associated with chemicals and metal engineering. The motor manufacturer, Renault, has a plant nearby and a railway connects Douai with Lille, Amiens, Saint-Quentin and Valenciennes. Douai is also known for its extremely rich coalfield, said to be the finest in Northern France.

The town has a considerable history and over the years its name has been spelt in different ways including the Anglicised version of Douay or even Doway. It is thought to have been a Roman fortress in the 4th century when it was known as Duacum. By the Middle Ages it was a thriving centre for the textile industry when it was part of Flanders. It became a French town in 1713 but suffered during the French Revolution and again in the two World Wars. There was considerable damage to the town during both wars but one of Douai's surviving and long-standing attractions is the Gothic style belfry that dates to 1380.

Standing 80m tall, it produces a highly enjoyable carillon of 62 bells spanning five octaves. The original bells, some dating from 1391, were removed in 1917 by the occupying German forces. Their intention was to melt them down for metal but this never happened and they were restored to the belfry in 1924. Their age was beginning to affect their sounds, however, and so in 1954, 47 of the bells were replaced. The chimes are mechanically rung every quarter of an hour but on Saturday mornings and Sunday mornings they are operated with a keyboard.

The town's impressive gate was constructed in 1453 with one Gothic face and the other of Classical design. It is known as the Porte de Valenciennes. The town's history is also complemented by the Benedictine Priory of St Gregory the Great which was founded in 1605 by St John Roberts of Douai. It accommodated a few exiled English Benedictine monks who started a college for Catholic boys from England, they being unable to receive a Catholic education in their own country. Apart from their studies in this school, they received tuition at the University. The English College was closed in 1793 due to the impact of the French Revolution and eventually in 1814 the monks returned to England—and settled at Downside Abbey in Somerset.

Some other English Benedictine monks formed the Priory of St Edmund at Paris in 1615 under the leadership of Dom Gabriel Gifford. He became the Archbishop of Rheims and Primate of France. However, those monks were also expelled from Paris during the Revolution but temporarily settled in the empty buildings that had been vacated by their colleagues at Douai. These monks later settled in England in 1903 where they established Douai Abbey near Reading. This also became an educational institution for boys until 1999.

Even more Benedictine monks returned from France to England in the aftermath of the French Revolution. They established a highly successful school for boys. These were the monks of Ampleforth in North Yorkshire, a community that could trace its direct lineal descent from Pre-Reformation Westminster Abbey. Like so many other English Catholic communities, they fled to France, but after being exiled by the French Revolution, they spent nine years at Dieulouard. In 1802, they were given a house at Ampleforth that had been built by Ann Fairfax of nearby Gilling Castle. It was for her chaplain, Father Bolton, himself a former monk of Dieulouard and although that house has now been demolished to make way for the construction of a new 'front door' to the Abbey (as one of the monks told me), it was the beginning of Ampleforth Abbey and College.

It is intriguing to think that when Father Postgate was undergoing his training for the priesthood, he would be familiar with many of the sights and sounds of Douai that can still be seen, heard and enjoyed. The town must have made a huge impression upon this young man from a remote village in the North York Moors and another point of interest is that, after growing up on a farm or smallholding probably with a very limited education in a very rural setting, his chosen career led to him living in a thriving and historic town in Flanders with its own university. There is no doubt he enjoyed and derived great benefit from his years at the English College but also from his association with this ancient town.

The university which housed the English College was founded in 1562 under the patronage of Phillip II of Spain because the town of Douai and its environs then belonged to the Spanish Netherlands. It achieved prominence during the succeeding decade because it was the focus of high education for English Catholics who were escaping persecution in their own country. The University had a strong English flavour because many tutors had come from Oxford also to escape persecution.

It was considered one of the most important institutions of its kind with five faculties taught with a distinctive Catholic flavour—theology, canon law, civil law, medicine and the arts. Within the University, however, there was also an Irish College, a Scottish College and houses for Benedictines, Franciscans and Jesuits. Later, subjects like philosophy and languages were taught, in particular Latin, Greek and Hebrew, with French added afterwards.

One of the former Oxford professors working at Douai University was Dr William Allen, later Cardinal Allen, who became Regius Professor of Divinity. When he realised there was scope for the establishment of a seminary to train English priests and at the same time educate them to university standards, he discussed this with a colleague, Dr Jean Vendeville, Regius Professor of Canon Law at the University of Douai. They agreed it was a viable and valuable idea and so the English College was founded in 1569.

In effect, this was a duplicate 'Oxford University type' of college away from England where it was educating priests who would be ready to cope with England's return to Catholicism. Indeed, the university's first Chancellor, Richard Smith, had studied at Oxford and had fled the persecution.

Without any regular income, however, the College relied on financial help from the King of Spain, the Vatican and private donations. Even with their assistance, the College was always short of money and conditions inside were far from ideal. The food was barely adequate, the buildings were not weather-proof, the furnishings were very basic but the students endured those privations as they worked for Christ and His Church.

When it was clear that England could not be swiftly re-converted to its ancient faith, the College began to educate and train missionary priests who would return to England in secret, there to keep the faith alive despite the threat of execution as a traitor. In 1573, the first 4 priests were ordained at Douai and they sailed to England a year later. By 1578, 75 had been ordained, out of which 52 returned to England.

This was the beginning of a steady flow of priests into England, all aware of the dangers to their lives but all equally devout and determined to re-convert the English and restore the old faith to their home country. But out of 300 or more priests sent from Douai to England by the end of the 16th century, more than 160 were executed with many more being imprisoned. Something like a further 160 were banished back to the continent.

Meanwhile the English College was expanding its work by publishing books and tracts, often of a very controversial nature. In 1609, it published its famous translation of the Old Testament together with the New Testament that had been produced at Rheims 27 years earlier. This became known as the Douai-Rheims Bible which was used continuously for more than three centuries. I am pleased to own a copy of this Bible although my edition was not published until 1796 in Edinburgh, when it was owned by a 21-year old woman called Mary Pearson. That surname is plentiful in Postgate Country.

It is worthy of record at this point that the English College at Douai also suffered from the impact of the French Revolution. Due to the war between England and France in 1793, the staff and students were forced to leave France. There is no space to record every factor surrounding that event except to note that after a tough time seeking suitable premises to house the College in England, the revived English College found a base in specially built accommodation near Durham.

It was known as Ushaw College which was established in 1808 and which itself celebrated its bicentenary in 2008. Sadly it had to close in 2011 due to a lack of student priests coupled with a fall in vital income. Ushaw's students are now trained at St Mary's College, Oscott near Birmingham and it is hoped that the former building at Ushaw may be used as a centre for Catholic Scholarship and Cultural Heritage under the auspices of Durham University's existing Centre for Catholic Studies (CCS).[1]

But all that happened long after Father Postgate had studied at The English College. At the height of its fame and importance, it was in that new, exciting and highly educated world that Nicholas Postgate found himself as a student. There is little doubt he would have received advance help and advice before leaving Egton for Douai and he would have been be assisted and advised by others who were familiar with the travel arrangements. There was a strong link between the people living along the Yorkshire coast and English Catholics then living on the continent. As early as 1583, for example, a Scarborough shipmaster was arrested for importing rosaries and vestments from the continent and in 1585 a shipment of 500 Catholic catechisms, 15 Latin New Testaments and other Catholic literature was intercepted and confiscated. At various points along the coast there were householders ranging from ordinary villagers to members of the nobility who were willing to shelter priests both as they assembled for embarkation to the continent and when they returned.

Sir Hugh Cholmley, owner of the Abbey House at Whitby was one of those who provided a safe haven for incoming priests after they had landed at Whitby, and Bagdale Old Hall was also said to have provided board and lodgings for missionary priests. This old house, which still exists, contained a priest's hiding place.

There was also rumoured to be an underground passage from the Hall to the harbourside but I have not found any evidence of that. Deeper inland, a number of country houses and farmsteads also provided shelter.

Not every incoming priest was safe, however. Two who arrived at Whitby from Douai (Edward Gennings and Alexander Rawlins) came ashore on an open beach near a high cliff, but when they arrived in Whitby town they were questioned by pursuivants but eventually found sanctuary at a safe house some three miles inland. However, both were later caught and executed as traitors—Edmund Gennings at Gray's Inn Fields in London (1591) and Alexander Rawlins on the Knavesmire a mile or so outside the walls of York on 7th April, 1595. These events occurred before the birth of Nicholas Postgate.

During the years closely preceding Father Postgate's birth, Cardinal Allen realised that the priests who had returned to England were in need of guidance and so in 1595 he appointed a leader. He was Father John Mush, a highly charismatic and business-like man who probably became the best known missionary priest in Yorkshire; he was also spiritual director of Margaret Clitherow of York, now Saint Margaret Clitherow. One of his tasks was to visit all the rest centres and safe-houses used by incoming priests, and sometimes known as clearing houses. His duties were to ensure they were safe and welcoming, with adequate food and rest facilities. Safety of the priests was of paramount concern.

Among the places visited and checked by Father Mush whilst in Blackamoor were Upsall Castle near Thirsk, Grosmont Priory and a farmhouse near Mulgrave Castle. There were lots of smaller properties which would later become familiar territory to Father Postgate, such as the Old Hall at Ugthorpe.

Against such a stirring and dangerous background Nicholas Postgate must have found his acceptance by The English College and his travel overseas all most exciting and very interesting, particularly after his years as a youngster on the North York Moors.

He entered Douai in July, 1621. Two references—the CTS pamphlet *Ven. Nicholas Postgate (1928)* and *Forgotten Shrines* by Bede Camm (2004 edition) both state that Nicholas Postgate was 'sent' to Douai to train for the priesthood. I searched for clues as to why he would be *sent* there, and by whom or why but found no answer, although Elizabeth Hamilton in her work *The Priest of the Moors* (1980) says that he *entered* the English College at Douai. That sounds more feasible![2]

It seems that the English College officials were very good at helping their students to travel from England to Douai, many undoubtedly doing so for the first time and with no experience of the world beyond their home areas. A priest from the College was therefore sent to accompany Nicholas Postgate to Douai. He was Father Francis Green. They were joined by two brothers who were also entering Douai as trainees. Thomas and John Tankard, like Nicholas Postgate, also came from Yorkshire and probably from Blackamoor. *Tankard* has various alternative spellings, perhaps the best known being Tancred. A Tancred family lived at Arden Hall near Hawnby deep in Blackamoor near Helmsley but it is uncertain whether the two trainee priests came from that branch of the family. There used to be an ancient nunnery on the site now occupied by Arden Hall. It was dedicated to St Andrew but was closed by Henry VIII in 1535. The ancient former Catholic Church at Hawnby, with parts of it dating from Norman times, contains several Tancred memorials and includes an inscription of Sir Henry Tankred (sic), this being dated 1620. That is only a year before Nicholas Postgate left Blackamoor to travel to Douai.

It is significant that these trainees travelled in pairs. It was the practice for missionary priests, where possible, to travel in pairs especially during a long journey into unfamiliar territory. This was part of their disguise—they would often appear to be a merchant and his clerk, or a well-off man travelling with his servant.

A student priest could enter The English College in one of two ways. He could be either an *alumnus* or a *convictor*. It was the custom at The English College that an alumnus could be educated free of charge, but he would have to contribute to his board and lodgings which was probably paid in advance through an agent in England. As an alumnus he was expected to contribute 300 florins for his course (£30 in modern value but a considerable sum at the time). We can compare this with a schoolmaster's salary at that time—he was paid around £4 per year. A convictor, on the other hand, was expected to pay all his own expenses, usually in advance before leaving England. Nicholas Postgate was a convictor because he was an adult.[3]

It is recorded that he entered the English College at Douai on 4th July, 1621, although the date of 11th July is also quoted.[4] He swore the College oath on 12th March 1623[5] and it is pleasing to think he might have had help from his mother who seemed to be wealthy enough to pay recusant fines but this is not certain. Perhaps he had another benefactor? The name of the aristocratic Smith family of Egton Bridge comes to mind. One practice was for the students to adopt an alias as a means of protecting their families back in England and so Nicholas called himself Whitemore, Whitemoor or even Whitmore. His alias was spelt in various ways but it is thought that Blackamoor, his home area, was the inspiration for this pseudonym.

Upon arrival he would have found himself within an extremely disciplined organisation with, obviously, a very strong emphasis upon the Catholic faith.

A working day began with Mass at 5am at which those who had not yet been ordained received Holy Communion. The Divine Office was said by all the students. His studies would include theology, philosophy and a full understanding of the Bible and its message. There was tuition in languages too, with Greek, Latin, and

Hebrew being dominant, and French being later included. Classical works in Latin were also studied and every Sunday and on feast days, each student priest had to deliver a sermon.

One aspect of the student-priests' leisure time—and perhaps as part of their curriculum—was to attend or even partake in plays and other dramatic productions, either with sacred or historical themes. I am sure that Nicholas Postgate's experience as a member of the Simpsons Players at Egton would have been beneficial in those cases, just as the priests themselves would occupy or entertain themselves in their various clearing houses—such as Grosmont Priory - upon their return to England.

Being older than most of the other students meant that Nicholas Postgate would inevitably find himself cast in the role of leader and it is perhaps significant that he remained at the English College for some time after his ordination. Perhaps he helped as a tutor to the younger candidates or assisted in the work of the College in other ways, for example as a sacristan? We have a flavour of his additional work for the College in its *Diary* which records '*magna cum fidelitate, diligentia ac Collegii emolumento*'. He worked hard, was of 'very fair character' and gave good service to the College.[6] He also gained an extraordinary reputation for piety and zeal.

On 16th September 1624, some three years after entering The English College as a very raw student, Nicholas Postgate sat the examination that led to his award of Minor Orders on the following 28th of December. He was promoted Sub-Deacon on 18th December 1627 and Deacon on 18th March 1628.[7]

He was finally ordained priest two days later on 20th March 1628.[8] He sang his first Mass on 2nd April that same year but remained at the English College for a further two years or so. This is probably when he is said to have given good service to the College. It can't have been an easy life there—the conditions were primitive by our standards and the students must always have been aware of the dangers facing them upon their return to England. There is no doubt they felt that God was watching over them as, like soldiers going into battle for their country, they returned to England.

During his studies, Father Postgate had a further trauma to endure—his mother had died in 1624 whilst he was studying at the English College. We have no record of whether or not he returned for her funeral or where she was buried but we do know that his eldest brother, Matthew, inherited the family property at Kirkdale. Apart from that, there are few surviving details about his family life.

And so, on the Feast Day of Saints Peter and Paul, 29th June 1630 Father Nicholas Postgate left the English College in Douai to sail back to Yorkshire to an uncertain future as a member of the English Mission. His task, as allocated by his tutors, was to be a travelling priest who would be in constant danger of execution as a traitor. Furthermore he had no home and no money but his duty was clear—he had to gather the English harvest.

It is not known by which port Father Postgate returned to England but, as his immediate future duties had already been agreed between the authorities in England and those at The English College, it can safely be assumed that he landed in Yorkshire, probably at Sandyford (Sandsend) near Whitby from where he could make excellent use of his childhood experiences in the moors and dales of Blackamoor. It was a regular practice for home-coming priests to be sent to their home areas.

As his parents were dead and his siblings surely dispersed to other localities, he would probably have no home to which to return. There is little doubt one of his first resting places after his trip from Flanders would be the quite substantial remains of Grosmont Priory, a place well known to him. From there after rest and refreshment, he would proceed to his first posting—which would be in the customary role as chaplain to a wealthy family. In this case it was a considerable distance from his childhood home in Blackamoor, but it may have pleased him that the start to his priestly career was to be in Yorkshire.

Ushaw College near Durham was the direct descendant of the English College at Douai. As restrictions against Catholic eased slightly towards the end of the 18th century, the war of 1793 between England and France meant that Douai had to close and this led eventually to the re-establishment of the English College on English soil. In 1808 it became known as Ushaw College and celebrated its second centenary in 2008; sadly, a lack of students for the priesthood has brought about the closure of Ushaw. Its functions have been transferred to St Mary's College, Oscott at Sutton Coldfield in Warwickshire.

Notes

1   *The Universe* (19 June 2011).

2   From 'The Doway Diary and Other Monuments' published following Father Postgate's martyrdom. (Leeds University Library).

3   *Ibid.*

4   See Father William Storey, *Ven. Nicholas Postgate* (London: Catholic Truth Society, 1928) and Dom Bede Camm, *Forgotten Shrines* (Leominster: Gracewing, 2004).

5   From 'The Doway Diary and Other Monuments' published following Father Postgate's martyrdom. (Leeds University Library).

6   *Ibid.*

7   *Ibid.*

8   *Ibid.*

CHAPTER 4

Homes and gardens

WHEN NEWLY ORDAINED priests returned to England from their continental training colleges, it was customary for some to become chaplains in the large houses of members of the gentry or aristocracy. From these fairly secure places they could minister to both the family who lived in the house and to the Catholics in the district. A large number of the gentry and aristocracy remained staunch supporters of the Catholic faith despite the fines and sequestration of their properties. Many of England's great houses had Catholic chapels constructed secretly within their walls and in addition, the houses or perhaps their outbuildings were often equipped with ingeniously constructed hiding places where priests could be concealed if the house was searched by pursuivants or parish constables.

It was also necessary for the priests to disguise themselves as servants, clerks or gardeners, and to adopt false names. This helped to protect them against arrest and eventual execution for being a traitor and it also protected their patrons against prosecution on charges of harbouring priests. The use of false names also protected a priest's family. Father Postgate adopted his mother's maiden name—Watson.

Whilst Father Postgate has, in our time, become widely known for his ministry in the remote wilds of Blackamoor in the North Riding, it should not be forgotten that he spent more than thirty years working in other parts of Yorkshire a long way from Blackamoor. That was about twice the length of time he strode around Blackamoor.

His first position after leaving the English College was as chaplain to Lady Hungate who lived at Saxton Hall in the village of Saxton. This is some four miles south of Tadcaster in what was then the West Riding of Yorkshire.

Today Saxton is a quiet upmarket village with some 250 residents, a long history—and a village pump! The remains of a Roman camp are close at hand and in Roman times vast quantities of high quality limestone were obtained from the nearby Huddleston Quarry, doubtless to construct their local fortifications, camps, temples and mansions. Indeed, most of Saxton's houses are constructed from this stone, making the smart, clean village look like one from Ryedale in North Yorkshire or even the Cotswolds. It has its dark side, however; a murder was committed here in 1933 but the killer was traced.

The beautiful golden limestone from Saxton's quarries has also been used through the centuries to construct many local churches and eminent buildings. In the 19th century, a remarkable fossil was discovered in Huddleston quarry. It depicted a hart's tongue fern which was almost four feet (120cm) in length. This fern has leaves that grow to between 10cm and 60cm in length, and some 3-6 cm broad, but without the fronds usually associated with ferns. In this case it had been solidified in a huge stone with a circumference of three feet (1m) and the enormous weight of more than 200 pounds (over 90kg).

Very close to Saxton is Towton Heath where the Battle of Towton was fought on Palm Sunday, 29th March, 1461. Although the site is on private land, the owner allows visitors to follow a marked trail whilst an information board provides the necessary data. The combatants were armies from York and Lancaster—the Battle of the Roses—and legend says that the red and white wild roses that grow around Towton Heath have sprung from the blood of the victims. Another story was that there was so much bloodshed that the water of the River Cock turned purple and the Wharfe, three miles away, was tinged with red.

Another famous battle was also fought in the vicinity. This was the Battle of Marston Moor (1644), part of the first Civil War, but yet another fight between warring parties of Englishmen. It is interesting to speculate whether Father Postgate ministered to the sick, wounded and dying at Marston Moor for it was fought only some ten miles away whilst he was serving at Saxton Hall. There is thought to be a long-forgotten chapel under the soil of the battle-field but searches have persistently failed to locate it. As I write these notes in 2011, a new campaign hopes to trace the chapel.[1]

Yet a further place of interest nearby is Lead Chapel that dates from the 14th century. Its predecessor on this site may date from as early the 9th or 10th centuries but since 1980, it has been in the care of the Churches Conservation Trust. Dedicated to St Mary (The Virgin Mary) and with a long Catholic history, it was allowed to become ruinous but was saved by a group of ramblers who organised its repair and on 6th November, 1932 it was re-dedicated as a Church of England chapel. However, a decline in population led to it being declared redundant. It is sometimes called The Ramblers' Chapel.

Hazelwood Castle is also within easy reach of Saxton and now (2011) it is a hotel and restaurant. It was the former home of the remarkable Vavasour family for some 900 years and their Catholic chapel was the only one during the Penal Times where Mass was permitted without a break. It served as the Catholic parish church for the area. It is claimed that Queen Elizabeth I personally exempted the family from the repressive anti-Catholic laws because she liked the Vavasours so much—but another story is that this family helped to pay for the naval ships that defeated the Spanish Armada in 1588.

The Vavasours sold the house in 1908 when it became known as Hazlewood Hall and it has since changed hands many times. It was a maternity hospital during World War II, then it became a retreat for Carmelite Friars from 1971 until 1996 and opened as Hazlewood Castle Hotel in 1997.

However, Saxton's own handsome stone-built church of All Saints is worthy of interest, particularly as it would be standing when Father Postgate worked in the village. Built and altered over the centuries and containing three medieval bells, its materials came from local quarries and it contains evidence of both Saxon and Norman construction. There is a thirteenth century triple lancet window containing modern glass, a fourteenth century chapel and a fifteenth century tower. Its age can be gauged by some medieval tombstones around it and the realisation that this churchyard contains the graves of some who fell at the Battle of Towton. Some twelfth century tombstones were re-cycled in the construction of the church tower and the graveyard contains a rare external tomb-chest of Lord Dacre who fell at the Battle of Towton.

There is no doubt Father Postgate would have seen and visited this church even if he was not allowed to celebrate Holy Mass there but inside there are memorials to the Hungate family, a clear indication of the Catholic origins and history of this old church. Indeed, earlier members of the Hungate family had added their own chapel to the church as early as c.1290, when it was dedicated to Our Lady, the Virgin Mary. It still contains an aumbry (a recess to contain vessels used in Mass) and also a piscina used to drain the water that had been used to cleanse the sacred vessels used during Mass. It was important that it drained into consecrated ground.

When Father Postgate took up his post in Saxton, he was chaplain to Lady Jane Hungate who was the third wife of Sir William Hungate. Sir William died in 1634, soon after the arrival of Father Postgate.

Thus Lady Hungate became a young widow with no children. She was the daughter of George Middleton of Leighton in Lancashire, the family to which Saint Margaret Clitherow of York belonged. The saint's maiden name was Middleton and she was executed in York by being crushed to death beneath tons of rocks, her martyrdom being on Good Friday, 25th March 1586, almost a century before the martyrdom of Father Postgate. Her place of burial is unknown but one site may be the ancient Catholic chapel of Stydd near Ribchester, Lancashire. Father Postgate was a devotee and whether he ever visited Stydd is not known but it did attract pilgrimages wishing to honour her. It is possible that his links with her family's descendants would have revealed the location of her grave—a secret to be kept. Another possible site is the Shrine of Our Lady of Mount Grace at Osmotherley.

Whilst serving as the chaplain at Saxton Hall, it is likely that Father Postgate adopted the disguise of a gardener along with his pseudonym of Mr Watson. He seems to have always used his true Christian name when adopting a pseudonym.

The role of gardener would be ideal because he was known to be a keen lover of plants and flowers—later stories are told of him pruning a pear tree at Pickering and growing daffodils around his tiny home near Ugthorpe—but during his time at Saxton Hall this would have been a very effective disguise. I am sure he would have tended the gardens at Saxton Hall and so it is sad that this house no longer exists. There are uncertainties as to where it actually stood but it may have been on the site of the present Manor Farm which has, above its doorway, the arms of both Saxton and the Hungate family.

Father Postgate's efforts to stimulate an interest in 'The Old Religion' appear to have been successful because, in 1633 during his time in Saxton, an entry in a Visitation Book at Saxton Church recorded,

> All the papists above meet at divers times together, some-
> times at Mr Francis Hungate house and sometimes at Jo
> Powells.[2]

It is quite possible that whilst serving at Saxton, Father Postgate
made occasional visits to Barnbow Hall, seat of the Gascoigne
family. This was a very ancient and important family who reputedly
had come to England in 1066 with William the Conqueror. One of
its famous members was Sir William Gascoigne, the Lord Chief
Justice of England who died in 1412, and the Gascoignes were close
associates of the Hungates. Indeed, Mary Hungate married Sir
Edward Gascoigne in 1726, the Gascoigne family making their
fortune from coal. One of the Gascoigne's seats was Barnbow Hall
close to Barwick-in-Elmet, famous today for its maypole displays.
The family was staunchly Catholic and their names appear on the
lists of recusants. Although one or two family members wavered in
their faith, most remained Catholic despite crippling fines and other
forms of persecution.

At the time of Father Postgate's mission in that vicinity, head of
the Gascoigne family was Sir Thomas, the second Baronet who in
1637 succeeded his father, Sir John. Two of Sir Thomas' daughters
joined the Church—Catherine became prioress of the Benedictine
Convent in Paris and Frances was a nun at Cambrai, the second
generation of Gascoigne daughters to do so. In a display of their
Catholic faith, whenever a Gascoigne was to be married, the banns
were read out at the market cross in Wetherby rather than the
Protestant church.

When Lady Anne Gascoigne died in 1661, an inventory was
made of the house and it listed 35 rooms, once of which was shown
as Mr Postgate's Chamber. Apart from this, there is no evidence
that the martyr ever stayed at the house and, of course, the name
of a room does not provide absolute proof. It is merely a suggestion
that he may have once been a guest.

Following the death of Sir William Hungate in 1634, Father Postgate continued his chaplain's duties at Saxon until the death of Lady Jane Hungate in 1642. He then transferred to Halsham in the East Riding of Yorkshire to the home of the 'old' Lady Dunbar. Halsham is in a very remote part of the East Riding not far from Withernsea but some five miles inland where the flat countryside tapers into Spurn Head. This is where the River Humber joins the North Sea and where the flat farmland is renowned for the constant breezes that blow off the North Sea. Coastal erosion is a continuing problem along the coastline. For Father Postgate, therefore, this district would be a dramatic change from the peace and tranquillity of Saxton and an equally dramatic change from his former life-style on Blackamoor's heathery heights.

The Constable family lived at Halsham from the 12th to 17th centuries, probably until 1620 but there were links with Egton Bridge. Those links were in the person of Sir Henry, the first Viscount Dunbar and husband of Lady Dunbar. Henry was the son of Thomas Smith of Bridgeholme Green at Egton Bridge. He had been created Viscount Dunbar in 1620 but died from wounds received at Scarborough during the Civil War. That was in 1645 so it seems that Viscount Dunbar was already deceased by the time Father Postgate arrived at Halsham, although it must be said that the precise date of his arrival is not certain. However, his home was in the residence of the Dowager Viscountess Dunbar, the Dower House of the Burtons of Burton Constable, namely the 'old' Lady Dunbar.

Halsham has long been regarded as the seat of the expansive Constable family and this was their principal home until they moved to Burton Constable Hall. The Dower House used by Lady Dunbar was about seventy yards from the present Halsham Church and I found signs of a moat in that vicinity.

The big house may have had a moat but it disappeared long ago although it was still being used as a Mass centre in the 18th century.[3] Also near the Church is a brick building, formerly a free school founded by the Constable family in Elizabethan times, whilst almost opposite the Church, at the end of a double avenue of conifers, stands a memorial to the Constables of that time. It is their mausoleum which is designed upon classical lines with a dome surmounted by a cross. It was built between 1790 and 1800 and taken into use in 1802.

It was constructed specifically to accommodate the remains of the Constable family. Most had left Halsham in the 15th century to live at Burton Constable Hall but many of their deceased members had been buried in the Chapel of St John of Beverley, built by the family on the north side of Halsham Church. Once the mausoleum was completed, however, their remains were transferred to a Catholic resting place. They are there today but Father Postgate would not have seen the mausoleum.

However, he would have noticed and surely visited the fascinating former Catholic Church at Halsham. With a pulpit dating to 1634, it is rich with architectural relics from almost every century since Norman times. Although it is built of local stone, there is much brickwork including the blocked arches at the north and south sides of the tower. I am sure Father Postgate would have mourned its loss to his ancient faith. Originally built without an aisle, one was added c.1170-1200, and in the 13th century the chancel was remodelled. A south aisle was added in the 14th century and an alabaster tomb-chest with an effigy dates to the 15th century. However, its fifteenth century sacristy was destroyed in the reign of Edward VI (1537–1553) probably at the time when the interiors of many parish churches were ransacked upon orders of the boy-king to remove or destroy evidence of their former Catholic use.

Inside Halsham Church, the remains of the smashed altar stone can be still be seen with some portions still bearing evidence of the five small carved crosses that adorned it as symbols of the Five Wounds of Christ. There is also a mutilated statue of the Virgin and Child, and another thought to be St Christopher. I am sure Father Postgate would have been horrified by this vandalism and wanton destruction because imagery of the Five Wounds of Christ was so important to him.[4]

I was intrigued by the skull and crossbones carved in stone above a door of this old church but could not ascertain its symbolism—except it might, in some way, relate to the Crucifixion. The site of the Crucifixion was Golgotha, the Place of the Skull and I was interested to find a similar but not identical carving on Saxton church.

But Halsham's remote church contains another puzzling item. It is a stone chair, and it has an arm-rest on the side adjoining what used to be the priest's doorway. Some authorities believe it is a Frith Stool installed for use by fleeing fugitives as they sought sanctuary. However, others disagree because, other than the sanctuary stools at Beverley Minster and Hexham, no other chartered sanctuary chairs are thought to exist. However, the church at Sprotborough near Doncaster in the West Riding of Yorkshire contains a 14th century stone chair with a carved man standing at one side and the head and shoulders of another with a forked beard. But like the chair at Halsham, this is not thought to be an official sanctuary chair or Frith Stool. The purpose of these chairs is therefore a mystery.

Father Postgate remained at Halsham until 1659, the year that old Lady Dunbar died, and from there he transferred as chaplain to a junior branch of the Constable family. This was at Everingham, also in the East Riding of Yorkshire. It lies about five miles west of Market Weighton and some 13 miles to the south-east of York.

It is a typically peaceful Wolds village but its big house—Everingham Park—contains in its grounds a splendid Catholic chapel for it was the seat of the Baroness Herries, Duchess of Norfolk and a descendant of a branch of the Constable family who had occupied the manor for more than four centuries. The altar in the Catholic chapel is made from Italian marble and in the nave in relief are scenes from Christ's life, with life-size figures of the Twelve Apostles. The chapel is in private ownership.

Its font is thought to date either from Saxon times or the Norman period but neither the house nor the chapel existed in Father Postgate's chaplaincy. The present Hall, built between 1757 and 1764, replaced the earlier one, but the chapel was not erected until 1836/39 and its presence was therefore never a secret. It was used as a Catholic parish church for the surrounding villages with regular masses until after World War II.

It seems that Father Postgate had made a splendid impression whilst chaplain at Everingham because many years later, when he was a missionary upon his native Blackamoor, he was invited back to Everingham Hall to join a family celebration. Apparently, the family had forfeited a substantial amount of their property under the Penal legislation, but had later recovered it, hence the celebration. Father Postgate joined the family for a meal and then in 1664 Sir Philip Constable left the sum of £5 to Father Postgate 'if still alive', and in 1672 another member of the family, George Constable, left him £1. Father Postgate signed a receipt for those amounts which has survived as one of his very few signatures.[5] According to Father David Quinlan in his Whitby Gazette articles (1967), a guest book was maintained at Everingham Hall and it contained Father Postgate's name.

The book was later placed in the care of Middlesbrough Diocese and lodged at St Hedda's Church, Egton Bridge but I have not found any further reference to it.

It was whilst serving at Everingham that Father Postgate was asked to be chaplain to both the Saltmarshe and Meynell families at Kilvington Castle and Kilvington Hall near Thirsk. This appears to have been the same family, with a member of the Saltmarshe family marrying a Meynell of old Kilvington Hall. This 'Kilvington Hall' was moated (I have seen the old map) and it was on the same site as Kilvington Castle. It seems to have been a single large building with two names, the Hall being developed from, or being part of, the ancient castle. The site is shown on Ordnance Survey map No. 91 at MR 851424. There are two villages, North and South Kilvington, the latter being much larger than the former. South Kilvington is about a mile north of Thirsk with North Kilvington's scattered farms and houses being another mile further north; the modern Kilvington Hall (1815) is about a mile north-east of North Kilvington. Both villages are within sight of Upsall Castle. The current Upsall castle was first built in 1872/3 but re-built in 1924 following a disastrous fire. It occupies a site close to ancient castle that was a safe-house for priests and stronghold of the Scropes. Two Lords Scrope of Masham and Upsall had their strongholds at the ancient Upsall Castle but the last of them died in 1349 and the old castle became ruinous.

A landowner called James Danby purchased the nearby land from the Constable family in 1653 and built the curiously named New Building which is now a farm that contains a priests' hiding place. The Meynell family were owners of the former Kilvington Hall with Sir Thomas Meynell, born in 1564, spending 15 years in prison for his Catholic faith He served his sentence partially at Hull (4 years) and then at York Castle.

It seems Sir Thomas died at the age of 83 some six years before Father Postgate arrived at Kilvington. 'Sir' was often a title given to a priest, so Thomas could have been a priest rather than a knight. Father Postgate was probably at North Kilvington from c.1660 until 1662.

My son and I visited Kilvington in late July, 2011. At South Kilvington the unhappy-looking cemented old church of St Wilfred, dating to the 13th century, contains evidence of its ancient Catholic history. It contains memorials to the Scropes of Upsall Castle whilst the huge font with its black marble bowl is said to have come from Scrope family chapel in the old Upsall Castle. There is also a holy water stoup and a niche where, before the Reformation, there stood a statue of St Wilfred but this would probably have been destroyed during the Visitation of Edward VI's commissioners between 1537 and 1553. It appears that this church itself was also subjected to Edward's desecration because in 1859, limewash was noted in the outlet of the piscina,[6] having remained for more than 300 years. Limewash was used to cover wall paintings of biblical scenes because they were considered idolatrous. They were in fact used as a teaching aid for people who could not read or write.

During our visit, we discovered that the current North Kilvington Hall was built in 1815 by Mr Thomas Meynell and was damaged by fire in 1972. It occupies a hillside site about a mile north-east of the old building. However, the old Kilvington Hall/Castle, where Father Postgate served as chaplain to the Meynell/Saltmarshe family, has vanished. The site is occupied by modern farm buildings belonging to Chapel Farm, North Kilvington. The farmhouse itself is of uncertain age but was probably built from the stones of the old Kilvington Hall, albeit with some later brickwork. It probably dates from the late 17th or early 18th century.

Of great Catholic interest, however, is the chapel from which the farm takes its name. The old chapel is sandwiched between the two ends of the farmhouse, each being a separate domestic household with the father's family at the southern end and the son's in the north. Externally, it is impossible to identify the chapel whilst inside, due to modern regulations restricting its use, it now serves as a storeroom.

This is the former Catholic chapel of St Anne which dates to 1690 and although one reference (*the British History Online—Parishes: Thornton-le-Street file*) states that the altar and pews are in position, this is no longer the case. The chapel would not have been used by Father Postgate because he died shortly before it was built. It served as the base for the Mission of St Anne and attracted a congregation from a wide area, with some families travelling by horse-drawn coach from York, some 25 miles to the south. The mission was transferred to Thirsk in 1867 upon the orders of Bishop Briggs. The church of All Saints in Castlegate at Thirsk was built in 1866/7 and is the successor of St Anne's Chapel of North Kilvington.[7]

For some years after the mission's transfer to Thirsk, St Anne's Chapel continued to attract a small congregation but everything except the holy water stoup was removed after the end of World War II when the chapel fell into disuse. When I called, the outline of the altar and location of the pews could still be seen but the font had gone and the gallery boarded up. The three large square-headed windows remain and they are located too high for inquisitive people to peer inside—from the outside, they look like normal but rather large house windows. Hanging above the altar during its time as a working chapel was a huge oil-painting of the Crucifixion. This was taken by the Meynells for display in Sts Mary and Romauld's church in Yarm, which the family had built in 1860.

Outside the chapel's west wall, there is a memorial cross bearing the names of eight deceased members of the Meynell family who died between 1844 and 1924. They are buried in a brick crypt beneath the memorial cross, and it lies immediately outside the chapel wall, very close to the back doors of the house. The current owner told me that when the contents of the chapel were being removed after World War II, a bone wrapped in silk was found under the floorboards where the altar had stood.

The owner's mother was present at that time and said later than four monks came from Osmotherley monastery and removed the bone but its fate or provenance is not recorded.

Coincidentally, the Catholic Church at Ugthorpe, known for its association with Father Postgate, is, like this chapel, also named after St Anne. She was the mother of Mary, the Mother of Jesus and therefore his grandmother, but very little is known about her.

However, it was to the old Kilvington Hall that Father Postgate came as chaplain to the Meynells around 1660. On the morning of his execution, young Mrs Meynell from Kilvington visited him in prison at York Castle. She was accompanied by Mrs Charles Fairfax who then lived in York and both found this an extremely harrowing and distressing occasion. The old priest, on the other hand, showed no signs of distress and was in surprisingly good spirits. Indeed, the women reported that he was cheerful. When meeting them on that last morning, however, he could see that both were pregnant and laying his right hand upon one of them and his left hand upon the other, he said, 'Be of good cheer, children. You will both be delivered of sons.' And so, in the fullness of time, they were—but sadly, both died in infancy.

Records do not show the Christian name of that Mrs Meynell, only naming the inheritors of the estates.[8] However, an Anthony Meynell died in 1665 aged 74.

He had married Mary, the daughter of John Thwaites of Long Marston, and they had six sons and seven daughters. The eldest son is named as Thomas but names of the others are not given. So could the Mrs Meynell who visited Father Postgate in York Prison on 7th August 1679 have been one of the daughters-in-law of Anthony, or perhaps the wife of a grandchild?

In contemplating Father Postgate's comparatively short time at Kilvington, which lies close to the western escarpment of Blackamoor, one can speculate that his presence there may have sparked a desire to return to his homeland. With some thirty years of his ministry being undertaken at a distance from the heather, the moors, the open spaces, the rivers and woods, we can perhaps imagine him seeing the purple heather on the hills above Kilvington and Upsall Castle, watching people going about their daily lives on those heights and scenting the brisk, fresh moorland air.

Furthermore, it was becoming increasingly difficult for the gentry to afford the luxury of a live-in priest—many were suffering greatly as they coped with crippling fines for not attending Church of England services. If they failed to pay the fines, their lands were confiscated by the Protestant State. A declining number of country houses were able to support a resident chaplain and so, in the active mind of Father Nicholas Postgate, it seemed that travelling priests were one solution to the task of maintaining the faith. Such thoughts, coupled with his time at Kilvington within sight of his beloved moors, may have prompted him to sever himself from the reasonably comfortable life of living in big houses with food and accommodation provided.

At the age of 62–65 or thereabouts, when most people are contemplating retirement or an easier life, Father Postgate decided to return to his moors. He had no wish to live in blissful retire-ment—he wanted to continue his mission.

He wanted to live among the poor as one of them, he wanted to help them, to make sure they had food, shelter and clothing, and they had had an opportunity to continue the practice the religion that meant so much to them and to him. But none of this would be easy because he had no home, no income and no-one to care for him. He would be alone on those moors in all their terrible and sometimes dangerous moods.

Yet in spite of all the hardships and difficulties that lay ahead, it was sometime around 1662–5 that he returned to Egton to begin his celebrated Mission of the Moors.

Notes

1   See *Yorkshire Post* (8 August 2011).
2   Elizabeth Hamilton, *The Priest of the Moors* (London: DLT, 1980), pp. 25–26.
3   *Ibid.*
4   See Chapters 2 & 3 above.
5   Father David Quinlan, 'The Father Postgate Story' in *Whitby Gazette* (17 February 1967).
6   William Grainge, *The Vale of Mowbray—an Account of Thirsk and its Neighbourhood* (Simpkin, Marshall & Co: 1859).
7   Quinlan, 'The Father Postgate Story'.
8   Grainge, *The Vale of Mowbray*.

CHAPTER 5

Other Places Widely Apart

OST OF THE early information about Father Postgate comes from Dom Bede Camm's *Forgotten Shrines* (1910) with a later Gracewing edition in 2004. In his chapter entitled 'A Martyr of the Yorkshire Moors', he writes of Father Postgate's chaplaincy at Saxton with the Hungate family. He also refers to his later chaplaincies at Halsham and Everingham in the East Riding with branches of the Constable family and follows with an account of his mission with the Saltmarshes and Meynells of Kilvington near Thirsk in the North Riding. None of these places is within the martyr's home district of Blackamoor.

However, Bede Camm adds a puzzling point. He writes that 'the martyr served at Kilvington Castle and Hall, (seat of the Saltmarsh and Meynell families) *and other places widely apart.*'[1] He does not explain where those 'other places' were or how he '*served*' there. I think that if Father Postgate had been a live-in chaplain in some other places, albeit disguised as a gardener, servant or clerk, then such a position would have been recorded, probably in the histories of the respective families. Even today it is possible that this kind of information could emerge when historic families donate their private documents to museums and libraries but in this case it would depend largely upon good fortune if such information was revealed.

I did wonder, however, whether the word '*served*' suggests that Father Postgate was not a live-in chaplain at other big houses but merely visited a range of widely-spread locations to either celebrate Mass, conduct a baptism or wedding, or perhaps a funeral. If this was the case, it would be done in secret and we would rarely, or perhaps never, be aware of it.

Perhaps, therefore, Bede Camm is right because we do know that the itinerant Father Postgate visited a wide area of the North York Moors, especially after he returned to the Egton area to further his mission on Blackamoor. It is equally certain that when attached to a great household as chaplain, his duties would take him into the neighbouring countryside to perform his religious duties. There is no doubt he would be constantly on the move, where-ever he served.

The CTS pamphlet *Ven. Nicholas Postgate* gives a hint of other posts as chaplain when the author states 'It would be a mistake to imagine Father Postgate as tied to one district'[2] although Elizabeth Hamilton in her book *The Priest of the Moors* does not state that he served with any other families and I have not found other sources to suggest that he did.

There is no doubt that the families with whom he served were well known to one another, usually being connected either by blood or marriage, and if he did serve as chaplain in places not recorded, then it may have been with one or other of their relations or friends. In selecting a resident chaplain, personal recommendation was vital because it affected both the priest and those he served. It may be that Father Postgate served with other families for very short periods. After all, he was latterly a travelling missionary priest.

The following Chapter 6 deals with his mission on the moors but we do know that Father Postgate visited other places, not necessarily to serve the local gentry. For example, it has been firmly established that he was involved with the Yorkshire Brethren, an organisation founded in 1660 for the welfare of aged and infirm priests. It was based at York. He was involved with the Brethren before he returned to Blackamoor and the organisation may have been created whilst he was serving at Everingham or perhaps Kilvington.

Although the Yorkshire Brethren was formed in 1660, its first General Assembly was not until 29th August, 1672 at Bootham Bar in York. By that time, Father Postgate had returned to Blackamoor some forty miles or so from York (as the crow flies) and it is not surprising that he voted by proxy through Christopher Barker, the Vicar General who worked in East Yorkshire. Although Father Postgate did not attend the first General Assembly, there is a record of him attending a second one at Peaseholme Green in York on 22nd November, 1676 only a couple of years or so before his arrest. A third meeting was held at a Mr Hunter's home in Petergate, York although it is not known whether Father Postgate attended. How he travelled to York, the duration of his journey and where he lodged are all unknown. The Yorkshire Brethren Fund remains active, however, and Blessed Nicholas Postgate is its patron.

As we have seen earlier, another interest that might have taken him beyond the Yorkshire boundaries was his devotion to the martyred Margaret Clitherow of York. She was canonised by Pope Paul VI in 1970 and there can be little doubt that whilst in York for the meeting of the Yorkshire Brethren Father Postgate would have taken the opportunity as a pilgrim to visit her former home in The Shambles. Known locally as The Pearl of York, Margaret was the wife of a butcher with premises in The Shambles and she was imprisoned six times for harbouring Catholic priests and allowing Mass to be celebrated in her home. When she was charged yet again for harbouring priests and permitting Mass to be celebrated, she refused to offer a plea to the court. It seems she took this stance to protect members of her family. The penalty was to be pressed to death beneath heavy weights placed upon her body on a platform, usually a door. This as known as *peine forte et dure* that literally means a severe and hard punishment.

It was used particularly against criminals who refused to plead and the idea was that, as the weight and pressure increased, so the culprit would be persuaded to make a plea. But Margaret Clitherow did not succumb. She died beneath those weights as her ribs and lungs collapsed. Her execution took place at the Tollbooth on the old Ouse Bridge which stood about fifty yards downstream from the present structure, and which was demolished in the 19th century. On Friday, 29th August 2008, a plaque to commemorate her death was erected by York Civic Trust at the Micklegate end of the present bridge.

Margaret Clitherow died on Lady Day otherwise known as the Feast of the Annunciation. That was 25th March 1586 which, at that time, was also Good Friday as well as being New Year's Day. It means she was martyred before Father Postgate was born and almost a century before he was also martyred. He would never know her in person except that her martyrdom would undoubtedly be a constant talking point among the Catholics of Egton whilst her home in The Shambles at York would have become a place of pilgrimage in his time—as it remains to this day.

However, there are indications that Father Postgate did visit Lancashire on occasions and although his links with the county may be very tenuous, he may have had a special interest in the ancient Catholic chapel of Stydd, said to be the secret burial place of Saint Margaret Clitherow. Another suggestion is that she was buried near the Lady Chapel at Osmotherley on the western edge of the North York Moors. It is more than likely that Father Postgate was also a pilgrim to the Lady Chapel particularly whilst he was chaplain at nearby North Kilvington.

However, there is another link between these two Yorkshire martyrs. On his return from the English College at Douai, we know that Father Postgate secured a position as chaplain to the Hungates of Saxton Hall near Tadcaster.

Lady Hungate was called Jane and she was the daughter of George Middleton from Leighton Hall near Carnforth in Lancashire. The Middletons were relations of St Margaret Clitherow and Leighton Hall was known as a hiding place for priests.

Indeed, every owner of Leighton Hall since it was built in 1246 has been a Catholic. Somehow they survived the fines.

Clearly, that part of Lancashire stubbornly refused to abandon the faith of its forefathers, so could Stydd have become a place of secret Catholic pilgrimage, even for pilgrims from far-off Yorkshire? If so, it is possible that Nicholas Postgate and/or other priests from the North York Moors were among them. Stydd is about twelve miles from Rawtenstall and very close to the Yorkshire-Lancashire border. The Lancashire medieval pilgrim centre was at Ladyewell close to Preston and some ten miles from Stydd—both are still actively patronised by Catholics and even Anglicans. We may speculate that Father Postgate was told about the secret burial place of Margaret Clitherow by the Hungates of Saxton.

However, another link with Lancashire may have arisen through Father Postgate's assistant, Father John Marsh. He was a Lancastrian but there could be some confusion over this man. A student of that name entered the English College at Douai in 1641 and was ordained in 1645, but the name was a pseudonym. Priests used false names to protect their families back home in England, and that priest's real name was John Wall. He used other aliases during his mission in England. Interestingly, he was also born in Lancashire in 1620 but does not appear to have returned to his native county. His work in England seems to have been confined to the Worcestershire area where he was arrested in December 1678 at Bromsgrove and later hanged, drawn and quartered. Coincidentally perhaps, he was arrested in the same month as Father Postgate.

The other John Marsh was Father Postgate's assistant for a time and it is interesting that a recusant Marsh family lived at Winstanley near Wigan. There were more Marsh family members living at Hindley in Lancashire. Several were Benedictine monks in the 18th century, but the family might also have produced secular priests. It is not clear when this John Marsh came to Egton Bridge but, after being educated at St Omer and Valladolid in Spain, he returned to England in 1660 as an ordained priest. He soon fell foul of a spy called Thomas Dangerfield. It seems that Dangerfield earned his money by tracking down Catholics, both priests and lay people, and then informing the authorities to claim cash rewards. He worked with the infamous Titus Oates in an effort to fan the flames of the so-called plot by Catholics and he impersonated the Duke of Monmouth whilst claiming miraculous skills at healing.

In April 1679, for example, Dangerfield was in prison pretending to be a Catholic convert as he sought to betray known Catholics—he was then using the name of Willoughby but in fact he was the son of a Roundhead attorney and a trained law clerk. It is evident that Dangerfield was trying secure evidence by which to incriminate Father Marsh and so the priest fled from London and first took refuge in Lancashire. Evidence of Father Postgate's links with Lancashire—if only through his assistant, John Marsh—may be seen in the Mass Posts that exist in Rawtenstall (see chapter 6) although I have not traced any records of Father Postgate actually visiting Lancashire. However, he was revered within that county (see 'Lancashire'—chapter 14).

Like so many Catholic priests of his era, Father Postgate was destined to work in his home territory but before then, we know he was a chaplain at Kilvington on the western escarpment of the North York Moors.

That meant he would be living only a couple of miles or so from Upsall Castle, a known safe-house and mission centre for travelling priests; it was also a stronghold of the staunchly Catholic Scrope family. It is highly probable that, from time to time, he would be a guest at Upsall Castle and he may have celebrated Mass there. Osmotherley on the western escarpment of Blackamoor has already been mentioned but its history is of Catholic interest due to its constant Catholic presence. On the plain below are the remains of Mount Grace Priory whilst on the edge of the lofty moors close to the village is the ancient shrine dedicated to the Virgin Mary. This is the Chapel of Our Lady of Mount Grace which remains a busy place of pilgrimage.

On its magnificent site on the plain below the shrine, Mount Grace Priory was said to be the only place in England in which the Carthusian plan in its typical form can be studied in existing remains.[3] The Carthusians differed from other Orders such as the Benedictines or Cistercians in that every monk lived a solitary life in his own cell, eating alone and seldom meeting his brethren except in church. They have been likened to hermits. Benedictines and Cistercians, for example, dined together and worked together in the fields or orchards.

Mount Grace Priory was founded in 1396 by Thomas, Duke of Surrey and it was dissolved by Henry VIII in 1535. The Chapel of Our Lady of Mount Grace is in the hills above this ruin and a vision of the Virgin was reported here centuries ago. A chapel was built to her honour in 1515 whereupon it became a thriving but highly secret pilgrimage centre. When pilgrimages were banned at the Reformation on the grounds they were superstitious or idolatrous, the chapel, for a time, ceased to be used. In fact it was almost demolished by the Reformers but the secret pilgrimages continued despite restrictions. Even as late as the reign of James I (1566–1625), pilgrimages continued, many taking place at midnight under cover of darkness.

Joseph Morris reports that the pilgrims were 'diverse and sundrie superstitious and popishlie affected persons' and we must ask whether they were due to the alleged presence of Margaret Clitherow's secret grave.[4] Today, pilgrimages are continuing and indeed increasing, albeit in the daylight hours. The chapel has been fully restored and is now cared for by the Benedictine monks of Ample-forth from their monastery in the village. This is the small Monastery of Our Lady of Mount Grace at Osmotherley that was opened in secret, probably in 1665. That was a dangerous period for Catholics but it was around the time that Father Postgate returned to those moors. We can speculate whether or not he was in any way involved in the opening of that secret monastery. The Catholic faith has never been absent from this moorland village with the current Mass centre and Chapel being on the top floor of The Old Hall. See Chapter 14 for further details of Osmotherley.

And so it was that when Father Postgate was at an age when most modern people are contemplating retirement and an easy life, he decided to abandon the relative comfort and safety he had enjoyed as a chaplain in a big house, and return to the harsh conditions of Blackamoor.

What prompted him to make such a dramatic decision is not known but I feel he may have wanted to return to his home area, particularly as his parents and other relations may have been buried near the old church of St Hilda that overlooked Kirkdale. Kirkdale must have held a treasure trove of memories for him and so it was around 1662-5 that he returned to Blackamoor to become a travelling missionary priest. He had no home, no money, no income, no transport, no family—but he did have huge faith in God. And so he headed directly towards his former childhood playground.

Notes

[1]   Dom Bede Camm, *Forgotten Shrines* (Leominster: Gracewing, 2004), p. 283.

[2]   Father William Storey, *Ven. Nicholas Postgate* (London: Catholic Truth Society, 1928), p. 5.

[3]   Joseph E. Morris, *The North Riding of Yorkshire* (London: Methuen, 1906).

[4]   *Ibid.*

CHAPTER 6

Return to Blackamoor

WE CAN MERELY ponder the feelings and emotions of Father Postgate as he returned to his family roots at Egton. He had been absent from Kirkdale in the depths of Blackamoor for more than thirty busy and memorable years but I am sure he missed the camaraderie and stimulus of Egton's renowned recusants. His parents had died, his siblings had dispersed and what became of his family home is not recorded. There is no trace of him returning to Blackamoor during his chaplaincies although he could have made secret visits, perhaps for important family reasons.

Another factor is that the inhabitants of the Egton area would have aged or died during his absence and some would have left the area. In returning, he would be almost a stranger with newcomers not knowing or recalling the name of Nicholas Postgate. If there had been no priests in the district, practice of the Catholic faith would have dwindled or even evaporated. It is most difficult to sustain the Catholic faith without the Mass, sacraments or priests but this area was fortunate in being served by priests who were heading inland upon their missions after arriving on the nearby coast. Many remained for a time at Grosmont Priory to serve the district.

There is little doubt that Father Postgate found it very strange to be back in the Kirkdale area especially as a venerable old gentleman without a home or family, and with no money or support. We do not know whether he requested his return or was ordered to do so and so we do not know what plans were made to receive him or accommodate him. Re-establishing himself, almost as a stranger, would be extremely difficult but he set about delivering his message with characteristic enthusiasm and determination. During the previous thirty years he had gained valuable experience and achieved considerable pastoral success that would aid him greatly in his new role. In 1664, probably just after returning to Egton, he wrote to Dr George Leyburn who was the current President of the English College at Douai, his term of office being from 1652 to 1670. Father Postgate informed him that, over the previous thirty-four years, he had worked in various parts of Yorkshire and reported he had conducted 226 marriages, 593 baptisms, 719 funerals and had brought 2,400 people into the Catholic Church. This complements his record whilst under training at the English College and adds to his stature as the holder of a Doctor of Divinity degree.

It has long puzzled students of his life and those who continue to live and work in the North York Moors National Park why a man with such a brilliant brain, undoubted charisma and in possession of so many talents whilst also being hard working and successful, should want to create such a dramatic and apparently downward change in his life-style. But Father Postgate knew what he was doing and was determined to succeed.

He made it known to everyone that he wanted to live as the poor lived, he wanted to be one of them to understand and care for them. He was prepared to conform to their diet, lodgings and dress. He wanted to devote himself entirely to the sick, tired, old and deprived people of all faiths or even those with no faith who lived on those remote and barren moors. He wanted Catholics to be enriched by regular Mass attendance and the sacraments sometimes after years of official denial. He wanted to be as near to emulating Christ's mission as was humanly possible. Even though the risks of being a

Catholic, especially a priest, were still present he could envisage a great future for the Catholic Church in England and its faithful members. But it would take a long time to achieve his aims and his mission would require stamina, hard work and an even stronger faith.

The fact he had been born and reared deep in those moors was a bonus. He knew the people, he could understand their character and personalities, he spoke their language and understood their dialect and local customs. He appreciated their fears and desires, and could help with their problems. Maybe he felt that life in big country houses was not conducive to portraying the actions and aims of Christ?

Whatever his innermost thoughts, his mind was made up. The precise date of his return is not known but was probably around 1662–5 and, as ever, his precise age was uncertain. Fired with a new enthusiasm, he sought accommodation near Kirkdale, his childhood playground, and it seems he was helped by a tailor called Posket who lived at Ugthorpe. This man was known for harbouring priests and may have been a relation but as a consequence, Father Postgate was offered the use of a tiny remote shack on the moors between Ugthorpe and Egton. In fact, it was about a mile from Westonby, a place he had doubtlessly visited whilst a member of The Simpsons Players and when he was living in Kirkdale. His new, but very modest home was literally on the doorstep of Egton's famous recusants' district in Kirkdale where he had played and prayed as a young man. In effect, Father Postgate had come home.

With only two rooms, one for sleeping and the other for living, but both very tiny at ground floor level, his cottage was built of moorland stone and was thatched, possibly with ling (moorland heather), but it had very low ceilings and a door that required a visitor to stoop upon entry. Inside was an earthen floor which may have been paved with uneven flat sandstone slabs or rounded pebbles. It has been said that the only thing that distinguished it from a cattle shed was a single chimney and very narrow lattice windows. The fire would burn either turf or peat—there were few trees on those moors. In summer there would be sunshine and long open views but in winter this lonely spot could be smothered in huge snow drifts and totally cut off from civilisation, sometimes for weeks on end.

The sad little cottage stood alone in the midst of heather-clad wasteland, open to the unfriendly weather of the moors but with long views down to the sea off the coast at Whitby. He was not to know, however, that in the years to come, Biggin House, only yards from his cottage, would be mentioned at York during his trial for high treason. The witness, Elizabeth Baxter, would tell the Assize Court how she had seen Father Postgate celebrate Mass at Biggin House.

It was said that one could see Mulgrave Castle from his cottage—not the present Mulgrave Castle but its sad predecessor. It is quite possible that Father Postgate had known about this deserted wreck of a house even as a child living fairly close to it but in his new role, he found it empty and available. It may have been a shepherd's shelter that had fallen into disuse. It is possible it was owned by the Radcliffes of Ugthorpe who would have readily granted him permission to make use of it, and it is also probable they accommodated him immediately upon his return to the area.

Despite the obvious drawbacks to such a remote and primitive shelter, it seems that the old structure was exactly what Father Postgate wanted and he put his own stamp upon it by surrounding it with flowers. Father Postgate was a keen gardener and had worked as such at some of the houses where he had been the chaplain; here, though, he planted wild daffodils and other flowers and, quite astonishingly, they flourished on that windy open space. It is claimed he introduced to Yorkshire from France both the wild daffodil and the Lenten lily; presumably many grew in the gardens he had cultivated at the big houses. In fact in England, the Lenten lily and the wild daffodil are different names for the same flower, although to slightly confuse matters there is a type of narcissus that is also known as Lenten Lily.

The wild daffodil is much smaller than its cultivated counterparts and the small wild daffodils that flourish in such profusion in several moorland dales are said to be descended from Father Postgate's crop around The Hermitage. In Farndale they are a tourist attraction around Eastertime, drawing visitors by the thousands, but they do thrive in other moorland dales. One legend is that Father Postgate planted a daffodil bulb every time a child was baptised into the Catholic faith, every time a couple were married, every time he received a convert into the Church and each time he secretly conducted a Catholic funeral, planting the bulb on the grave following a secret night-time interment. That may be why so many daffodils grow on moorland churchyards, particularly Protestant ones. Those bulbs would be planted in widely scattered places and, of course, they would flourish and reproduce.

When Father Postgate was martyred no-one else inhabited that lonely cottage and so when the pilgrims came to visit his old home on the moors after his execution, they helped themselves to the daffodils and their bulbs. The result was that they no longer grew to his memory in that isolated place. The daffodil, of course, represents spring and renewal, and its yellow colour is also the symbolic colour of the Five Wounds of Christ (chapter 2). Sadly, the old Hermitage, sometimes called Postgate House or simply Mr Postgate's, was demolished in 1870 but an oak beam was saved and tiny wooden crosses were made from it. They were given to the people of Egton and Ugthorpe and some still exist. It is claimed that a wooden armchair on display in St Hedda's Church at Egton

Bridge came from this old house. However, its provenance is doubtful.

The site is occupied by a large farmhouse still called The Hermitage (and which was formerly occupied by my cousin) and it stands within sight of the A171 Whitby-Guisborough moor road near its junction with Lealholm and Egton lane ends. The only surviving remains of Father Postgate's old house are some stones from his living room wall that have been re-used in the building of an outer wall in the lowest of three linked parts of the farmhouse.

But if Father Postgate was seeking a private retreat for contemplative moments, his devotees soon became aware of his hide-away and set out to visit him, perhaps for nothing more than a piece of advice but also perhaps to have a child baptised or a wedding arranged. In fact, he did not have to fend for himself because a lady from Ugthorpe called Jane Harris who was probably organised by the Radcliffe family, would 'do' for him—she would go to clean his house, deal with his washing, make his meals whenever he was at home and even made communion hosts for him to carry during his rounds. I am sure she also kept the keenest of pilgrims at a respectful distance!

There is no doubt he would say Mass on occasions at his humble abode but he would also have the freedom to use Ugthorpe Hall, the home of the Radcliffes. It was fitted with one or perhaps two hiding places for the shelter of priests if the place was raided by pursuivants. A cow-byre was used for Mass and contained a holy water stoup and aumbry which is a small recess or cupboard in a wall to store sacred vessels and items used at Mass. There is no doubt other safe and secret locations in or near Ugthorpe were used for the celebration of Holy Mass and probably to hide priests.

Whenever anyone arrived at Father Postgate's home on the moors, either by prior arrangement or unexpectedly, he would make them welcome, and if they brought him offerings such as food, money or even clothes, then he would always share them with people in greater need than he. His benevolence and calm nature endeared him to all who encountered him, even those not of his faith and so he quickly gained a following to become known as The Good Samaritan of The Moors.

As the number of Catholics increased due to his ministry, it became evident that he required more space and more locations in which to celebrate Mass. His Mass centres were in private homes and farms or even in the open air if no building was available but in all cases the services had to be conducted in utmost secrecy. A priest who was caught by the authorities whilst saying Mass was deemed to be a traitor to England and upon being found guilty would be executed by being hanged, drawn and quartered, a legalised form of human butchery.

The celebration of the Catholic Mass, therefore, in addition to baptisms, weddings and funerals which had been forbidden by law since 1559, had to be conducted in conditions of total secrecy and much of that depended upon the wisdom, alertness and discretion of the local people. Indeed, as Father Postgate went upon his rounds he always dressed as a gardener by wearing a brown tunic shaped rather like a monk's habit, and in winter a white cape made from canvas. His cape offered protection against the harsh weather but also served as a disguise in snowy conditions.

As an additional form of security he continued to use his pseudonym of Nicholas Watson. He took with him the tools of his trade to aid his disguise and is often depicted carrying a stave—perhaps that was a hoe with a narrow tip? There is no doubt he spent many nights away from home, sleeping in a barn or perhaps even a cave in a wood or a hollow beneath an outcrop of rocks. He refused to use a horse or pony to help him undertake long journeys—he felt that a horse or pony would be a sign of wealth and so he rejected all such offers, walking everywhere. He must have covered thousands of miles on foot and perhaps his only sign of weakness or a health problem was a throat condition that resulted in a fairly persistent cough. To ease it, he grew a beard which would help to keep his throat warm against the chill winds.

Whilst on the constant look-out for suitable Mass centres, there is one story that he made use of a secret chapel at Fyling Old Hall near Robin Hood's Bay.[1] However, he was given the use of a suitable house some four miles from Ugthorpe. It stood half-way down the steep hill between Egton and Egton Bridge and it is likely he began to celebrate Mass there in 1665. It was a single storey building of stone with a thatched roof and it stood on a piece of elevated land known as Brown Hill from where a view of Eskdale included seven or eight villages. The site is very near the present Anglican Church of St Hilda at Egton but the house now occupying that position is not the original even though its south-facing wall contains a stone bearing the words 'Mass House'.

The original faced east therefore its front elevation appeared to be at the back; what was in fact the rear of the house overlooked the road that runs downhill into Egton Bridge. The old stone building was very small inside and comprised a living room and pantry with two bedrooms on the ground floor but above the bedrooms there was a tiny loft lit by a small window. It was barely visible beneath the overhanging thatch, and not readily visible from the road because it faced east. Access to the loft was through a trap-door via a step-ladder that was removed when not required, and the loft occupied a space above the two bedrooms. Its total area was 15 ft (4.5m) by 10 ft (3m).

However, much of its limited space was taken up by the trap-door whilst the height between the floor and the thatched roof was less than six feet (2m); Bede Camm reports it was only 5 ft. 6ins high (1.65m), barely enough for a person to stand upright. Indeed, the entire house could accommodate very few people so when Mass was celebrated in the loft there was room there only for the priest, an altar server and perhaps two members of the congregation.

Other worshippers would have to remain on the ground floor since the old house could not accommodate many of them, but it is thought they could hear the progress of Mass. However, the ringing of bells and the singing of hymns would probably not be undertaken because they might attract the wrong kind of interest from parish constables or pursuivants.

That tiny loft, which served as the secret oratory for Father Postgate, contained a rather unusual feature. It was an escape route for the priest in case the house was ever raided by pursuivants. Downstairs, it formed part of the larger bedroom, being built into its south-east corner so that, from inside, it appeared to be part of the structure of the house. That apparently harmless piece of stonework concealed a vertical shaft that led down from the loft above and opened into an adjoining out-building. The escape route was large enough for Father Postgate to use for any urgent departure and he could flee through the out-buildings and into the woods where he could safely hide. This probably indicates that he was a small man. The children in St Hedda's School at Egton Bridge were often given exciting accounts of his remarkable escapes from here—there were times it sounded as if Robin Hood was fleeing from the Sheriff of Nottingham! It was all very exciting stuff for impressionable young lads who would then play chasing-style games involving the fleeing priest and the nasty pursuivants. It was at Egton in 1666, during Father Postgate's time, that a local man called William Kirk of Eskdaleside was charged with sedition for saying of soldiers in a public house at Egton,

> Theire Major is growne so high that he saith never a papist shall weare a sword, nor so much as a stick in his hand: I say never a Cavalier shall weare a sword; within a few days thou shalt not see a king in England.[2]

The little secret oratory at Egton was used regularly by Father Postgate even though his mission took him far away into the wilds of Blackamoor. It was, in fact, his permanent little church although he also ministered over a huge area containing other Mass centres, and so, when he died it fell into disuse. In time, people forgot all about its past history and the tiny secret oratory was never mentioned even though the building was always known as The Mass House. It seems also, that the door into the loft was never opened for years and in time, the presence of the oratory was forgotten.

Then in 1830, an amazing thing happened. A servant girl decided clean the upper part of the living room wall, but the fragile plaster gave way beneath the weight of her hand and the astonished girl found herself gazing into what appeared to be a church in miniature. The altar was set out for Mass, the vestments laid ready and there was even a missal, candlesticks and crucifix in place. Fortunately, the tenants, Mr and Mrs Harrison, were Catholics and doubtless aware of the history of their home and its links with Father Postgate who had been executed 151 years earlier. He had never returned to celebrate Mass which was laid out ready and waiting in their loft.

No doubt stunned by this discovery, they reported it to Bishop Penswick, the Vicar Apostolic of the Northern District. He came to inspect the discovery and decided to leave some of the relics with the Harrison family. They retained the tabernacle door, the portable altar stone and two crucifixes one of which contained an unspecified relic. Bishop Penswick then took away all the other treasurers which, to my knowledge, have never been listed and their whereabouts are now unknown.

The tabernacle was an especially cut hole in the wall of the loft but it had a door complete with a frame. This was left in position upon Bishop Penswick's departure but sadly, the Harrisons were visited by an Anglican priest who pretended he was a Catholic, and the family were persuaded to part with the tabernacle door.

For years, its fate was unknown although its frame remained in place until the death of Mr Harrison aged 99. Now, however, the tabernacle door is in St Hedda's Church at Egton Bridge, its past whereabouts something of a mystery. The oak step ladder into the loft was removed too and cut up to be made into lots of small crosses; when I was at school in Egton Bridge, I was told that most households in the area possessed one of these crosses and I believe that whenever a member of the Harrison family was married, they were given something that had been found in the loft on that day in 1830. It means, of course, that most of the relics have been widely dispersed and their provenance has undoubtedly been lost.

However, Father Postgate's portable altar stone has been preserved. This was one of three that he is known to have used and in this case it seems he left it permanently at The Mass House. When the contents of the secret oratory were dispersed, the resident Harrison family were allowed to retain that stone which was marked with five small crosses, one at each corner and one in the centre—the emblem of the Five Wounds of Christ.

When the new Catholic Chapel was built at Egton Bridge in 1797/8, it was one of the first in Yorkshire if not England following the relaxation of restrictions against Catholics. That was due to the Catholic Relief Act of 1778. The chapel was dedicated to St Hedda (Haedde), a monk of Whitby Abbey and Bishop of Winchester, a man of whom the Venerable Bede wrote: 'he was a good and just man who in carrying out his duties was guided rather by an inborn love of virtue than what he had read in books'.[3]

The new chapel was built on land donated by the Smith family of Bridgeholme Green in 1797, and the building included both a new chapel and a priest's house. It also included a small bell-tower even though bells were forbidden on Catholic Churches—the idea was to be ready for another change in the law whenever it happened. In 1850, the Harrison family donated the altar stone to the St Hedda's Chapel and later when the new and present church was built in 1866–67, the stone was let into the altar of the Lady Chapel where it remains today (see chapter 14). It is a direct link between Father Postgate and this mighty church, called by some the 'Cathedral of the Moors'. The former chapel was then converted into the school where I was later taught my three Rs, with the Headmistress addressing us from the former pulpit. There is no doubt that the generosity and support given by the Smith family of Bridgeholme Green contributed greatly to the status of Egton Bridge as the village that ignored the Reformation whilst being part of the renowned 'Bishopric of Papists'.

The old Mass House survived until 1928 when it was declared too dangerous to survive as a dwelling house and so it was knocked down. I believe the local people secured further pieces of oak from the ruins and from the loft ladder which were made into treasured objects such as small crosses. They were distributed over a wide area and the locations of some can be found in Chapter 14.

But if Father Postgate's secret oratory has been lost and his relics dispersed, his impact survives in the moors he knew as Blackamoor.

Notes

[1]   Father David Quinlan, 'The Father Postgate Story' in *Whitby Gazette* (17 February 1967).
[2]   John Leyland, *The Yorkshire Coast and the Cleveland Hills and Dales* (London: Seeley and Co, 1892).
[3]   St Bede, *Ecclesiastical History*, Book 5, chapter 18.

CHAPTER 7

Witch Posts or Mass Posts?

WITH A 'PARISH' covering around 553 square miles—1432 square kilometers, the area of the North York Moors National Park—and with no transport other than his own two feet, Father Postgate was compelled to spend lots of time away from home if he was to serve his growing congregation. If the people could not come to him, he would have to go to them and there is no doubt that those living some distance away found it extremely difficult, if not impossible, to regularly attend his Mass centres. The short answer was that he needed more centres.

His massive, lofty and bleak parish lacked the high number of Catholic gentry houses to which he had previously become accustomed but he did find several spacious and suitable houses and farms. He lost no time persuading their occupants to allow them to become Mass centres whilst continuing the need for absolute secrecy.

As I was later born and reared in the area in which he served, I can confidently say that it was that action by him (and the secrecy that surrounded it) that gave birth to a curious piece of moorland folklore. The lore suggested—and continues to suggest—that the North York Moors contain a unique collection of objects known as witch posts. With a few exceptions at Rawtensall in Lancashire, original witch posts were found only within the North York Moors. They are part of a seventeenth century inglenook hearth but are not found in every house that boasts such a hearth.

Clearly, there was some kind of selection and because these objects are so unique and decorative, it is not surprising there are imitations and replicas, plus a surprisingly number of fakes. The Museum of Witchcraft at Boscastle in Cornwall displays decorative imitations but no replicas or genuine posts. These imitations cannot be mistaken for copies or replicas of the genuine moorland posts.

So what are witch posts? And how are they associated with a Catholic priest of the Penal Times? A witch post requires a strong upright piece of oak which forms part of a seventeenth century inglenook fireplace. The post appears to support the huge bressumer directly above—that is the long beam that spans the entire house to support the smoke hood. The post also supports the heck partition at the side of a short passage leading from the living areas into the cross passage beyond and thence out of doors. Thus the correct title for such a post is heck post although some are referred to as speer posts.

Figure 2: Detail of a witch post

A witch post is therefore a heck post but one that is readily distinguished because it bears a large carved X on its upper face. In addition to the X-mark, the post may carry other carvings, perhaps something connected with the family, love symbols, signs of the Zodiac or other markings. However, most of them also bear, immediately below the X-mark, a number of carved scrolls, sometimes called billets. The number differs from post to post.

There is no doubt that the presence of such posts within a few selected houses did—and still does—raise questions about their purpose. In the absence of a feasible explanation, they have become known as witch posts and are named as such in books and articles about folk lore or in literature specifically relating to the North York Moors and the village of Rawtenstall in Lancashire. They are also named as such in the *Dictionary of English Folklore*[1] and in many other reference or topographical books that feature those areas. It was thought they were installed to protect the household from the activities of witches.

It is difficult to determine how many posts were created. I know that some were destroyed but I believe it is possible that others are awaiting discovery.

To my knowledge, however, seven are still in their original houses with a further six in museums (as at autumn 2011). Ryedale Folk Museum at Hutton-le-Hole near Kirkbymoorside contains three genuine posts, Whitby Museum has one and Pitt Rivers Museum in Oxford has two, all of which were originally installed within houses on the North York Moors. I have also received reports of a dozen or so that featured in moorland houses but which no longer exist and I regard that information as reliable. Furthermore, it is known that many were removed or destroyed possibly by Methodists, because they were considered pagan symbols.

So what have witch posts to do with a travelling Catholic priest? It is my contention, after several years of research, that these posts have nothing whatever to do with witches but everything to do with Father Postgate's mission on the moors.

The folk lore surrounding them has provided an effective smoke-screen for some three and a half centuries. It could even be the case that during Father Postgate's moorland mission, house-holders were questioned about the curious post on the hearth and to disguise its true purpose, they would say it was to deter witches. In the prevailing anti-Catholic climate, that was a wonderful cover story but it has now entered moorland folk lore where the alleged witch links are now believed to be true.

So why do I believe these posts are associated with Father Postgate? We can date them to the mid-seventeenth century or later because, in the early or mid-seventeenth century, there was a period of house-building on the moors that became known as The Great Re-Building. This happened in other parts of the country too. Rather primitive medieval-style houses with thatched roofs, wattle-and-daub walls and earth floors with a fire in the centre of the house where smoke filtered through the thatched roof were demolished in favour of stone-built houses with improved facilities.

In those earlier houses, people slept at one side of the large central living area, and livestock lived at the other side, all under the same roof. The Great Re-Building, which made good use of the waste materials from the earlier houses, provided far more comfort-able homes known as long-houses. Many still exist. Even if the roofs continued to be thatched, the living quarters were divided from the livestock's accommodation by a thick stone wall against which a new-design of hearth was built. The hearth supported a massive hood which guided the rising smoke through a primitive chimney instead of allowing it to filter away through the thatch.

The fire burned continuously against that wall—it was con-stantly required to provide heat, light and cooking facilities but also provided a form of central heating for the living area by heating the stones of the wall. This was wonderful in the winter months. Salt boxes and spice cupboards were built into those walls so the contents were always dry and free running when required—bliss for a busy housewife.

The structure of the fireplace (see illustration below) was dominated by a huge beam that spanned the house at about head height to rest upon each of the outer walls. This was called the bressumer.

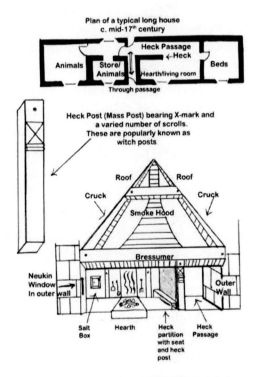

Plan of a typical long house c. mid-17th century

The heck passage, which leads into the cross passage, may be on the left or right of the hearth

Figure 3: Fireplace with heck post

At one side of the hearth—either to the left or right—a short passage led into a second longer passage known as a through- or cross-passage. This cut through the width of the house and had doors at each end. Whilst threshing the corn with flails in that passage the doors at each end were opened and the through-draught blew away the waste chaff. That is why our house entrances are known as thresholds.

Beyond that cross-passage was the new livestock area under the same roof as the living area. These long houses remain a feature of the moorland scenery—Father Postgate was arrested in one of them—and many have inglenook hearths still in regular use.

In modern houses, the livestock's accommodation is now set apart from the domestic quarters, and the former stables, cowsheds or pigsties have been converted for household use.

In every new long house, a partition of wood or stone was built between the heck passage and the hearth to provide shelter from draughts. On the inside of that partition there was usually a fireside seat. For the people of the time, this was comfort indeed. An example of both an early medieval house and a long house with such a fireplace can be viewed in Ryedale Folk Museum at Hutton-le-Hole in North Yorkshire. The differences are readily visible. The long house on display is a genuine mid-seventeenth century house known as Stang End and it was moved stone by stone c.1968 from Danby-in-Cleveland and re-built within the museum grounds. And this house contains a witch post which I now believe to be a Mass post (see figure 4 below).

Every known original Mass/witch post formed part of one of those mid-seventeenth century inglenook fireplaces. Mass posts were not built into the hearths—the blank posts were already *in situ* before the Mass posts were created by cutting an X mark—a saltire—at the front near the top. Other personal features were

added, often by the householders. The post in Stang End bears a
wooden peg—this was added in 1946 from which to hang towels!

Figure 4: Inglenook at Stang End, Danby-in-Cleveland.
This entire house is now in Ryedale Folk Museum

In many houses there are heck posts and speer posts without
any carvings or decorations and some are locally known as *witching
posts*. I think this comes from the old belief that all such fireside
posts were installed to deter witches. Witching posts are neither
Mass posts nor witch posts. They serve no known purpose.

Down the centuries, these posts have been subject to much
speculation and many theories, the most common being that they
are made of rowan wood (mountain ash) because their perceived
purpose was to ward off witches.

At the height of witchcraft fears, rowan was considered the finest deterrent; it would have made sense to harness the power of the rowan to create witch posts.

However, the genuine 'witch' posts are *not* made of rowan. With the exception of a replica post at Egton (which is not part of the hearth) all the originals are oak, as are many replicas. That is beyond question. I think the notion that witch posts were made of rowan arose because people *expected* them to be made from it due to its ancient role as a witch deterrent. Furthermore, until recently many posts bore a thick greyish-white coat of limewash. This was a wood preservative and a pesticide but as each new coat covered the previous one, it was difficult to determine the type of timber beneath. As a consequence, the people who later lived in those houses (especially after the persecution of Catholics ceased) assumed (wrongly) that the posts were made of rowan wood. Superficially, the witch theory seemed logical.

However, modern cleansing methods have revealed that they are made from oak. Oak wood was not used as a witch deterrent although its leaves and acorns were thought to protect people against evil. The tree was also sacred to the pagan Norsemen and Celts.

In addition, we must also bear in mind that if the X-marked posts had been witch deterrents, they would have appeared in many more homes but also in livestock shelters through-out England and not only within the Moors. We may think of them as having the same function as lucky horseshoes—horseshoes, being metal, were thought to deter witches and so they appeared on virtually every house, cattle shed or stable throughout England. Even today, brides carry model horseshoes during their wedding ceremonies. Witch posts don't have that kind of universal acceptance—they are unique to the North York Moors and one village in Lancashire.

For centuries, witchcraft beliefs were widespread in England but the so-called witch posts have no medieval or pagan history. They did not appear until the mid- or late seventeenth century after inglenook hearths had become so popular throughout England. It means we can date the appearance of these X-adornments with some accuracy.

Indeed, the name *witch post* did not appear until the nineteenth century—Canon J. C. Atkinson's book *Forty Years in a Moorland Parish* (1891, revised in 1908) gives space to witchcraft beliefs and old houses on the North York Moors but does not mention witch posts. However, he does refer to a heck post with curious carvings that was suspended from the beam above it.[2] It was hanging from the bresummer, probably because its base had rotted. However, in 1893 he donated an X-marked post to Pitt Rivers Museum in Oxford. With a dozen scrolls, it came from the Old Shoemaker's Shop at Danby-in-Cleveland, deep inside Blackamoor, and his letter dated 5th March 1892 describes it as 'the (assumed) witch post.'

I have seen his letter and it is clear he did not believe the posts were genuinely associated with witchcraft—but he does not offer an alternative suggestion although I suspect he recognised their true purpose. That is maybe why he donated one to a museum in far-off Oxford! I wonder from time to time whether he knew about Father Postgate's mission on the moors but did not want to highlight it in his books—and I also wonder whether he ever visited the Mass House at Egton.

Joseph Ford's *Some Reminiscences and Folk Lore of Danby Parish and District* (1953) tells us that such posts *came to be called* witch posts suggesting this was not their original name. Other authors believe the term came into use during the middle years of the 20th century. In other words, witch posts were unknown when witch-mania was at its zenith so if these objects are not connected with witch lore, what are they?

Joseph Ford, a devout Methodist, provides an important (and perhaps the first) clue. He writes about witch-laying ceremonies in what he describes as 'our forefathers' time' and criticises the parish priest for not doing enough to eradicate superstition. He adds that people distressed by family problems would seek help from the parish priest. He suggests the priest would then 'lay the witch' and adds, 'When this mysterious ceremony was over… it was the custom of the priest to cut the Roman figure X on the upright oak post…' Here he was referring to the local Catholic priest, with Canon Atkinson confirming that 'priests' were Catholics and 'Church priests' were Anglican.

The transmission of this information by word of mouth down the generations has probably distorted some of the facts, but it is likely the *mysterious ceremony* was something like a Catholic house blessing conducted in Latin with candles and holy water but not necessarily linked to the X-cutting ceremony. Certainly it would be mysterious to a non-Catholic of the time, and also to Mr Ford's Methodist ancestors who, in later years, listened to such stories. However, Mr Ford does tell us that the X became known as the priest mark, even if his ancestors mistakenly thought it was a device for deterring witches.

It is very significant that these fashionable new hearths were in place within their inglenooks when Father Postgate was carrying out his priestly duties around those same moors. At this point, I will issue a reminder that Father Postgate had great devotion to the imagery of The Five Wounds of Christ. It had long been used as an international symbol of Christian resistance to tyranny (see chapter 8). It is not difficult to imagine that whenever a house was offered as a place in which he could safely celebrate Mass he would bless it (hence the mysterious ceremony!) and then cut the abbreviated symbol of The Five Wounds of Christ on a convenient piece of timber.

That symbol was the X on the heck post. In that way, a house was secretly identified as being blessed or perhaps selected and deemed safe for the celebration of Mass or other Catholic services such as baptisms and weddings. There is no doubt Father Postgate would also have blessed some of those houses with inglenook hearths for no other reason than they were new buildings but a blessing alone might not have warranted an X-mark. I think the X indicated that Mass was celebrated in that chosen household. This could explain the scattering of X-marked posts around the Moors on routes surely used by Father Postgate. There were at least three in the village where I was born, and others in Egton and Egton Bridge where I attended school.

So once Father Postgate had selected and marked (with his X) a house as being suitable for Mass, how did the faithful know which one, out of several over a very widespread area, was the one at which the next Mass would be celebrated? Regular changes of venue were vital if raids by the authorities were to be avoided, consequently any house used for Mass could not bear external marks that might be noticed by the pursuivants and parish constables. If people spoke about the next venue, they were in danger of being overheard which could lead to a raid followed by fines or even arrest. Strict secrecy was vital which meant the identity of the selected house had to be made known by a secret code. And so Father Postgate—or one of his assistants—devised a system of secret messages that were visible from a great distance but which would mean nothing to a parish constable or even a spy. Spies and informers did exist at that time but in the locality there nothing more ordinary that washing being placed out to dry on a hedge or perhaps spread across the heather.

This is where the scrolls on the posts become highly significant. They numbered anywhere between one and twelve—within one district there would have been no two posts bearing identical numbers of scrolls.

It does seem feasible that Father Postgate would have divided his huge 'parish' into several smaller units because some posts do carry an identical number of scrolls but the relevant houses can be up to 25 miles apart. Indeed, two at Egton bear a single scroll, one having been transferred to Whitby Museum whilst the other is in the roof of the bar of the Horseshoe Inn at Egton. It can be seen there now, serving as a roof support. Useful and unwanted pieces of solid dressed oak were always in demand for structural work, particularly as lintels. There is no doubt that when 'witch' posts were removed, many were recycled as lintels. It is possible that the Horseshoe post was brought from elsewhere to serve its present purpose or of course, the house that originally contained it may have no longer been used for Mass. Incidentally, this inn still has a splendid inglenook hearth in daily use.

However, local Catholics were familiar with the houses in their locality and knew the codes on the heck posts. So what did the codes mean?

In his CTS pamphlet *Ven. Nicholas Postgate* (1928)[3] Father William Storey gives a very strong clue. He writes:

> More quickly and more surely that any other messenger, the sheets signalled where Mass was to be said. Spread out as if to air on the hedges by the cottage, their number indicated the spot in the neighbourhood that had been selected.

Thus the message presented by the white washing was simple. Two white sheets, towels or cloths indicated that the house with two scrolls on its heck post was the next venue—if four sheets were displayed, they would indicate the house with four scrolls and so forth. It was a secret unspoken system that would work today. In fact, some of the scrolls do resemble neatly folded pieces of washing such as pillow cases or towels! However, some posts do not bear scrolls or billets; I can only think a secret number would not be necessary due to the isolated situation of the post.

Alternatively, the post could have been the first one created in a particular area, where others were not considered necessary. Father Postgate would not require such posts at his earlier missions in Saxton, Halsham, Everingham and Kilvington because he celebrated Mass there in secret chapels although I am sure symbols would be used to indicate the time of Mass. The same could apply to Ugthorpe where he regularly said Mass at The Hermitage and Ugthorpe Old Hall, and occasionally at Biggin House. There were clutches of posts in Eskdale between Egton Bridge and Danby with others scattered around the moors and they were upon routes that would have been used during Father Postgate's long journeys from his home at The Hermitage.

So what about the posts in Lancashire? How can they be explained? They are all at Rawtenstall and when I visited the village, I was told there was only one witch post. In fact, I found five, two of which present rather a puzzle because, although they present similar information to those on the moors and elsewhere in Rawtensall, they are very different in appearance. The question is: how and why did those X-marked posts appear in Lancashire if Father Postgate's mission was centred upon the North York Moors, many miles to the east of both Lancashire and the Yorkshire Dales?

The answer might be that Father Postgate secretly visited Lancashire on occasions, perhaps as a pilgrim at Margaret Clitherow's shrine—but we cannot be certain that he ever made such a journey. Another matter to consider is that he had several assistants whilst working on the moors. Many were priests coming back to England after training on the continent, and some remained to help him, basing themselves at Grosmont Priory.

We don't know the names of all, but we do know of Father Thomas Goodricke who had been born in the North Riding and who had also attended the English College at Douai, returning to Yorkshire in 1631. He was never heard of again after 1669. Another was Father John Jowsie, a native of Guisborough on the northern edge of Blackamoor; he was also educated at Douai and it is known he was somewhere in Yorkshire in 1648. He was last heard of in 1678. Another assistant on Blackamoor was Father John Marsh. He was a Lancastrian who occasionally travelled back to Lancashire from Egton Bridge. It is said he looked after himself whilst living in rooms at Bridgeholme Green, by invitation of the Smith family.

Perhaps Father Marsh was responsible for emulating Nicholas Postgate's secret symbols at Rawtensall, a community not known for its toleration of Catholics at that time? If Father Marsh had seen or experienced the X-code system in operation, he would surely wish to emulate it in his native countryside. As I write these notes in the later autumn of 2011, I am sure further posts will come to light in and around Blackamoor.

At this stage, I should add that the famous Pendle Witches of Lancashire cannot be linked to the so-called witch posts. The trial of those alleged witches was a shocking miscarriage of justice that featured the appalling death of some simple women. All were found guilty and hanged at Lancaster Castle on Thursday, 20th August 1612 when Nicholas Postgate was about twelve years old.

One was a devout Catholic called Alice Nutter who was arrested on Good Friday. She refused to give evidence or to reveal her intended destination and was therefore arrested and executed as a witch. It is claimed, however, that she was on her way to a Catholic Good Friday service with her family but if she had told the authorities where she was heading, her entire family would have suffered.

Many believe her selfless actions were those of a martyr; indeed, some members of her family were Catholic priests and martyrs.

Before I continue the story of Father Postgate's work on the moors, it is perhaps time to reflect upon what inspired him to make use of the internationally recognised imagery of The Five Wounds of Christ in the remote acres of the North York Moors.

Notes

[1] Jacqueline Simpson and Steve Roud, *A Dictionary of English Folklore* (Oxford: OUP, 2000).

[2] See Canon John C. Atkinson, *Forty Years in a Moorland Parish* (London: MacMillan, 1891, revised in 1908), p. 454.

[3] Father William Storey, *Ven. Nicholas Postgate* (London: Catholic Truth Society, 1928).

CHAPTER 8

The Five Wounds of Christ

BEFORE CONTINUING THE account of the life and work of Father Postgate, it is important to consider the wider relevance of the X-mark used by Catholics both in his time and earlier. It will now be appreciated that this has a strong association with his moorland mission and it is a reminder of his presence that can still be seen in private houses and museums more than three hundred and thirty years after his death.

Over the centuries, the X-mark appeared as a rallying emblem, a symbol of resistance to a new and oppressive authority and as a symbolic sign of re-assurance during the Penal Times. It was an image to which the young Nicholas Postgate was regularly exposed through his contacts with the Simpsons of Egton (see chapter 2) and it would have undoubtedly exercised considerable influence upon him. Not only would he see the emblem on the banners and flags of the Simpsons, it would also appear on historic churches and upon sacred images both in England and overseas. I am sure he would encounter it whilst at Douai and he also refers to the Wounds of Christ in the hymn he wrote in York Castle as he awaited execution (see Chapter 13).

In addition, coded messages, songs and carols, often with a subversive element, were commonplace at that time - for example, *A New Dial* or *The Twelve Days of Christmas*. One that was altered in the aftermath of the Reformation, probably in 1625, and sung by Catholics as a rallying cry, remains a well-known carol and is titled *Green Grow the Rushes Oh*. Each verse relates in some oblique way to religion, ranging from God (*I'll sing you one, Oh*) via *four* for the gospel makers, *ten* for the commandments and *twelve* for the apostles. The other numbers might not be so easy to work out, but verse five is very relevant to the world of Father Postgate because it reads:

I'll sing you five, oh,
Green grow the rushes, oh,
What is your five, oh?
Five for the symbols at your door,
Four for the gospel makers, etc ...

The *five symbols at your door* are those which appeared on safe houses where travelling priests could obtain rest and refreshment. They were often five scratches in the X form. They were also carved on all altar stones whether portable or permanent and even today if one examines surviving altar stones in ruined abbeys and old churches, the five crosses can be easily identified—one in each corner and one in the centre to form their own X mark.

The Five Wounds of Christ were those suffered during the crucifixion but also the wound caused by the spear that pierced His side to determine whether He was alive or dead on the cross. In some portrayals of that image, His hands and feet are spread-eagled with His heart in the centre, whilst other images comprise only the shaft of the spear crossed with the shaft of the stick that carried the sponge of vinegar to His lips during His final moments. When His heart took the place of the spear wound on many images of the Five Wounds, it later became an icon in its own right—we know it as The Sacred Heart of Jesus.

In all the variations of images of the Five Wounds of Christ, there is a clear outline of the X-mark. The portable altar stones carried by Father Postgate during his mission on the moors bore such symbols—a small cross (+) scratched in each of its four corners with another in the centre. Three altar stones are recorded—two now in St Hedda's Church at Egton Bridge and the third in St Joseph's at Pickering.

In fact, it was the practice for all altar stones to bear the symbolic Five Wounds of Christ as the form of X marks but the requirement for an altar *stone* containing the relics of a saint ended with Vatican II.

I am now going to include an article written by a senior Buddhist monk who is perhaps better known to me as my son, Andrew.

The Five Wounds of Christ by Ajahn Punnyo

The Tudor chronicler, Edward Hall, gives a vivid, if somewhat partisan, account of the Pilgrimage of Grace (1536). This was a rising in Yorkshire against State restrictions imposed on Catholics and was led by Robert Aske. The pilgrims, sometimes referred to as soldiers, included some of the greatest landowners in Yorkshire such as Lords Darcy, Latimer, Lumley and Scrope along with the Catholic Archbishop of York and many hundreds of ordinary people. They marched south to prevent the wholesale destruction of their Catholic faith and actually captured York and Hull.

They adopted the Five Wounds of Christ as their banner but the pilgrimage was doomed. Henry VIII double-crossed the pilgrims and some 220 rebels were ruthlessly executed, including Robert Aske. At one point in his account, Hall wrote:

'The soldiers had a certain cognizance or badge embroidered or set upon the sleeves of their coats which was a representation of the Five Wounds of Christ.'

That representation appeared in many other places: (for example see St Cuthbert's cross in Durham Cathedral that can be viewed as either a + or a X). Some splendid examples occur in the stained glass windows of the Benedictine Priory Church of Great Malvern.

They date from 1440 and depict both the Five Wounds of Christ with the hands, feet and heart, but also the crossed shafts of the spear and vinegar stick. The latter present a particularly strong and clear image of the X-mark. The image also appears on the devotional card of the Carthusian monks of Sheen in Surrey where the Five Wounds are arranged in their usual saltire form and depicted on a shield. The shield is superimposed over the spear and stick with its vinegar sponge, once again in the form of a saltire cross. Further references occur in *'The Three Orders: Feudal Society Imagined'* by Georges Duby in the chapter dealing with the Tudors, the Reformation and the Crusades.

When the northern rebels began to gather in Pontefract on 22nd October, 1536 as a prelude to the Pilgrimage of Grace, one of the groups, from the lands of the Bishopric of Durham, wore distinctive insignia. It was the Black Cross of St Cuthbert in cruciform shape - but also a badge showing the Five Wounds of Christ. This was a wounded heart in the centre with blood dripping into a chalice with two pierced feet below. When the castellan of Pontefract Thomas Lord Darcy saw the badges of the Five Wounds it reminded him of the same device he had used during an expedition to fight the Moors of North Africa in 1511.

Others had accompanied him, including Sir Robert Constable and Sir Ralph Ellekar. Darcy remembered that somewhere in Pontefract Castle was a store of the badges he had used and so the storeroom was searched and the badges recovered. He presented one of them to Robert Aske, leader of the Pilgrimage of Grace.

Badges and banners depicting The Five Wounds had been used during the Crusades too, and so it was considered apt that similar crusades could also be utilised against Henry VIII and Elizabeth I for their alleged heresy.

It was seen as right and just that rebels fighting for their religion in England could make use of the symbols used during those historic crusades to the Holy Land. It was regarded as a legitimate form of civil disobedience against a heretical establishment.

Lady Margaret Beaufort, Countess of Richmond and mother of King Henry VII (1457-1509) also made use of the Five Wounds of Christ on what she called the Arms of the Passion. To reflect her devotion to Christ, she displayed a shield bearing an image of the Wounds and it contained a 'bede' of gold. This is a close association with the colour yellow.

What interests me is the yellow colour. Many images of the Five Wounds, even those with flesh coloured sections and coloured backgrounds, appear yellow when viewed from a distance but in the Great Malvern case the large heart is yellow. The significance of this, when considering the X-marked posts, is evident in Chapter 2 where we learn the yellow X was used by the Simpson players in their Catholic skits—with the young Nicholas Postgate probably a member. Even as a very young person, whether or not he participated in their plays and interludes, he would have been aware of its form, image and powerful potency, prob- ably due to the folk memory of generations of recusants in his native Eskdale and also through his attendance at their performances, probably in Grosmont Priory.

Yet another depiction of the Five Wounds is the Jerusalem Cross that formed what became known as the Crusader Cross. This comprised a large cross (+) coloured red with smaller crosses in each of its four quarters and cross members on the tip of each of its arms.[1]

In his book *Forgotten Shrines* Dom Bede Camm refers to the Rising of the North (1569), which he describes as a second Pilgrimage of Grace, and refers to Markenfield Hall near Ripon. He writes 'The great courtyard, now so peaceful and deserted, was once filled with armed men each with a crucifix hanging from his breast and a red cross upon his arm, grouped beneath the banner of the Five Wounds of Christ.'[2]

This second uprising had adopted the powerful emblem of the first and Bede Camm also refers to one of its members, Sir Richard Norton of Norton Conyers near Ripon. He was 71 years old and described by the writer William Camden (1551–1623) as an old gentleman with a reverend grey head bearing a cross with a streamer. In his words 'The Norton's ancient had the cross and the Five Wounds of Our Lord did bear.'[3]

There is no doubt the impact of these emotional uprisings lingered in the folk memories of all northerners, especially Yorkshire folk. Stories of bravery and determination would pass down through the generations, ensuring their sacrifices were never forgotten.

In 1615/1616, some years after the Rising of the North, a youthful Nicholas Postgate, reportedly aged 13, was involved with a company of Egton-based strolling players and actors called The Simpsons. Whether or not this was the martyr Father Nicholas Postgate is unclear. Other families called Postgate or Poskett lived at Egton and also in the locality but the name Nicholas is not duplicated in recusancy records although an older Nicholas Postgate was living at Sleights some five miles from Egton. Despite this uncertainty, the balance of probability indicates that this is indeed the martyr in his youth—after all, we do not know the precise date of his birth.

It is not known for how long the young Postgate had been one of their troupe but some boys joined as early as age seven. The players had a reputation for staging rebellious skits and parodies that criticised the new State religion but their activities were by no means restricted to Egton and district. Indeed, in 1609, they staged the first known performance outside London of William Shakespeare's 'King Lear'.

In his article 'Players of Interludes in North Yorkshire in the early seventeenth century', G. W. Boddy wrote of a court hearing resulting from a performance of '*St Christopher*', on Candlemas Day, 2nd February 1609.[4] It was at the splendid home of Sir John Yorke, Gowthwaite Hall in Nidderdale in the West Riding of Yorkshire, more than fifty miles from Egton even as the crow flies. That gives some indication of the distances covered by the strolling players of Egton at a time when travelling was far from easy, particularly over long distances.

According to G. W. Boddy, Saint Christopher was a version of an old morality play with a cast of nine. In itself, it was quite harmless and inoffensive. That was the standard version that might be safely played in a Protestant gentleman's house. The Simpsons, however, had an extra Catholic version into which an interlude was interpolated. It was this interlude that caused the scandal that led Sir John Yorke to being incarcerated in the Fleet Prison in London. The apprentice, Thomas Pant, in his questioning at first denied that there had been any seditious interlude, as did William Harrison, Edward Whitfield and the other players but by that time of the trial, Pant had left the company and was more vulnerable to pressure than the others. He later testified that there was indeed an interlude and corroborated the evidence of William Stubbs, a Puritan minister and justice for the Fountains Abbey area, who had gate-crashed the performance.

The interlude took the form of a disputation 'counterfeyted betwixt him that plaid the English Minister and him that plaid the Popishe priest toucheing matters of religion'. The minister argued on the basis of the Bible but the priest countered that it was not enough and held up the yellow cross. 'The minister (did) show forth his said booke or Byble to defend his profession withall, and that it was rejected and scoffed at,' alleged Stubbs. Sir Stephen Proctor (the Puritan patron of William Stubbs) described how 'he that plaid the foole (William Harrison) did deryd the minister'. When the minister was condemned or overcome, 'there were flashes of fire cast forthe and then he that plaid the Divell did carrie the Englishe minister away.'

Clearly there was an enormous fuss and a lot of anger about the seditious content of this interlude and another witness, William Bourne, spoke of an actor who played a Catholic priest who 'had a cross on his shoulder, one in whyte like an anngell...' It was believed that one of those who played the devil was Christopher Yorke, the son of Sir John; Christopher later became a Carthusian monk.

There is little doubt the play in Gowthwaite Hall was the social event of the year in Nidderdale, being attended by a huge audience of tenants, servants and neighbours, young and old. Most were Catholics for whom such events provided comfort and uplifting moments in their fight to keep their faith alive and these plays gave them confidence, even though the content of the plays (often written by Christopher Simpson senior) appeared ominous and seditious to men like Proctor and Stubbs.

From the point of view of Sir Stephen Proctor, the Nidderdale play presented an opportunity to exact his revenge on Sir John Yorke and as Proctor was acquainted with Sir Thomas Posthumous Hoby of Hackness it was easy to identify the troupe of players as the famous or perhaps infamous Simpsons from Egton. As a consequence, warrants were issued, these resulting in court appearances for the players and Sir John's eventual imprisonment.

The home village of the Simpsons—Egton near Whitby - was described as the most Catholic-minded in the North Riding of Yorkshire and it was here that both the Simpsons and Nicholas Postgate grew up. It is likely that Christopher Simpson senior, leader of the troupe, received his early education from Edward Nickson, an Egton schoolmaster, but also from William Postgate, a retired farmer who also taught children. He was probably the grandfather of Nicholas and it is possible that the young Simpson acquired his love of drama and acting during those early formative years.[5]

The Nidderdale performance was typical of the content of such plays and performances and during their tours and performances it is evident the Simpsons made effective use of the symbolism of the Five Wounds of Christ. Whereas the Five Wounds had been the rallying sign for earlier generations of persecuted Catholics, now they were being resurrected in a new form, albeit retaining a loyal Catholic following in spite of adversity.

Christopher Simpson and his brother Robert (or uncle—the records are not clear), were both ardent Catholics who defied State orders to conform to the Church of England. Both were recusants with Robert being described as 'a turbulent recusant' and they persistently refused to attend Protestant services in the old St Hilda's Church at Egton. It has been replaced with the Egton Mortuary Chapel.

That old Pre-Reformation St Hilda's church was savagely knocked down in 1876 to make away for the present building. As it was demolished, the font was unceremoniously thrown down the hillside but was later recovered and placed in either the new St Hilda's Church at Egton or St Mary's Anglican Church at Goathland. It is not clear which! Some of the woodwork from the old church is now in Delves Cottage, Egton Bridge, the location of an X-marked post and more of that woodwork is in other local houses.

It seems the play-writing and acting skills of the Simpsons was due to their close association with the Hodgson family of Priory Farm at Grosmont. Only a mile or so from Egton and within Egton parish, this occupied the remains of the former priory destroyed by Henry VIII's commissioners in 1535. Trainee priests, when attending the English College in Douai, took part in music, plays and sketches and some of them, freshly out of Douai, stayed in the safe house at Grosmont Priory Farm when they returned to England. The dilapidated state of the former priory buildings contained a rest house and meeting place, along with a priests' hiding place and a secure secret escape route down to the River Esk. So entrenched were the Catholics of the area, that John Ferne, secretary of the Council of the North, claimed that Sir Richard Cholmley of the famous Whitby family could call upon 500 men to protect his interests. Sir Richard was the main sponsor of the Simpsons. Richard, a powerful man, was the son of Sir Henry Cholmley, Lord of the Manor of Whitby and was grandson of the eldest daughter of the first Earl of Cumberland; he was also related to the influential Scropes of Wensleydale.

Egton parish included Grosmont Priory which was considered a breeding ground for sedition and a deliberate flouting of the anti-Catholic laws. As such, it attracted the attention of Parliament, the English establishment and the Sovereign.

The Simpsons' Players were always on the lookout for signs and symbols that would express their resistance, and there is no doubt the one that would encapsulate the deeply felt conviction of all Catholics, particularly northerners, would be the banner or badge of the Five Wounds of Christ in one or other of its forms. The Simpsons had discovered that when the badge appeared in any of their plays or interludes, it had an electrifying effect on the audience. The image itself could be considered seditious and dangerous to those who understood its significance. Little wonder, therefore, that the actors used the cross that signified the Five Wounds. The actor who played the priest in the *St Christopher* interlude wore a cross on his shoulder, and each of the soldiers in the Rising of the North wore a red X-shaped cross upon his arm, yet another symbol of the Five Wounds of Christ.

As a result of the impact of the Douai priests in encouraging the dramatic talents of the Simpsons at Grosmont Priory Farm, it is of interest that Nicholas Postgate entered the English College at Douai in 1621 to train as a Catholic priest. There can be no doubt he had earlier been strongly influenced by the rallying power and potent imagery of the Five Wounds of Christ. This was something he was to bring into his own ministry on the moors many years after leaving Douai as a priest. However, he would not make rash use of a rousing and seditious banner because it was the custom of travelling priests to flit in and out of sight like wraiths. For this reason, it is more likely he, and perhaps other priests, would make use of a hidden symbol—but one that nonetheless portrayed Christ's sacrifice on the cross.

It would be wise to create a less blatant, less dangerous version of the Five Wounds, one that was disguised for use in the Catholic underground of the period.

On the badge used in the Pilgrimage of Grace there are clear colour representations of the two wounded hands, two wounded feet and the Sacred Heart of Jesus, all arranged in the shape of a saltire or St Andrew's cross. It is an arresting and graphic image. When viewed from the middle distance, the flesh-coloured components blur into a yellow X-style cross. That simple yellow cross could then be an ideal symbol of Catholic resistance that was instantly recognisable to a Yorkshire recusant, but merely appearing as a yellow cross to a Protestant or an officer of the State. It is interesting and of some significance that the Puritan minister, William Stubbs, described a yellow cross being held up during the

Simpson's seditious interlude at Gowthwaite Hall in 1609. In the interlude the 'priest' uses the yellow cross to counter and trump the arguments presented by the protestant minister.

Symbolically, therefore, the sketch looked forwards to the long awaited victory that had not yet been realised following the Pilgrimage of Grace or the Rising of the North.

On the banner's badge, there is also the representation of a chalice supporting the Sacred Host within which is held the Sacred Heart of Jesus. In addition to representing the crucifixion, therefore, this symbol also indicated the Eucharist or the celebration of communion, the focal point of the banned Catholic Mass.

If Father Postgate, in the latter years of his ministry on the North York Moors (c.1662 until 1678) was looking for a symbol or mark for a house where Mass was celebrated, a simple disguised adaptation of the famous badge would be ideal. The simplest way would be to reduce it to a mere X.

In fact, the traditional symbol of the Five Wounds of Christ had for centuries been a pentagram, a five pointed star. The Roman Emperor Constantine, the first Christian emperor of Rome, used the pentagram in his seal and amulet.

Before the crucifix became such a powerful symbol, the pentagram was the preferred symbol to adorn the jewellery and amulets of early Christians and would be combined with an X or a phoenix, the phoenix symbolising the triumph of life over death. The Pilgrimage of Grace and the Rising of the North each used a more graphic depiction of the Five Wounds that showed the nails in the Hands and Feet, and the wounded Heart. Nonetheless, that symbol could easily be disguised as a simple X cross—and any Catholic who saw it would appreciate its significance.

Still in existence is a graphic medieval version of the Five Wounds found on a wooden boss in the roof above the chancel steps of St Tudno's church at Llandudno, Wales. This is a vivid reproduction in colour which, from a distance, appears in the shape of a yellow X. Perhaps a more acceptable example is the yellow emblem of the Five Wounds in St Marie's Catholic Cathedral in Sheffield.

One disadvantage of simplified versions of the Five Wounds is that the evocative chalice in the original examples is lost. However, with a little imagination combined with the fact that there is often at least one scroll or horizontal line both above and below the X-marks on cross posts, it is easily seen that it becomes a double for the absent chalice: $\overline{\underline{\Xi}}$. Representations of a chalice are often in the form of a simple X, perhaps slightly elongated.

With a few deft strokes of a saw, therefore, Father Postgate could create on a hearth-side heck post a symbol that simultaneously performed many functions—housing blessing, a symbol of Christ's passion and crucifixion, of the Mass and of the resistance as shown in both the Pilgrimage of Grace and the Rising of the North.

However, the organisers of the Pilgrimage of the North and the Rising of the North, along with Father Postgate in later years, were not the first rebellious Yorkshiremen to form a loyal devotion to the Five Wounds of Christ.

In the early years of the fifteenth century, Richard Scrope, the Archbishop of York, refused to accept the authority of the usurper King Henry IV. Scrope, a Yorkshireman to the core, had preached in York Minster that it was the duty of all Englishmen to rise against the King, adding that he would bless them for so doing. Copies of that sermon were sent to every church in Yorkshire—all Catholic at that time—and resulted in hundreds of disgruntled northerners arriving in York. Quite unintentionally, Archbishop Scrope found himself riding at the head of hundreds of rebels and heading for a rendezvous at Shipton Moor, some seven miles north of York. The year was 1405. Henry lost no time in dealing with this unruly archbishop—he was tricked, betrayed and arrested by the King's

Men and a swift execution followed. It took place in a cornfield between York and Bishopthorpe but before being beheaded, Scrope asked that he receive not one wound but three, in the name of the Five Wounds of Christ. For years afterwards, it was said that corn in that field grew more richly than any other around York.

This long term devotion by Catholics to the Five Wounds of Christ had associations with being 'hidden away' or secretive, something of relevance to a missionary priest of the Penal Times and his congregation of recusants. Medieval mystics, including Julian of Norwich talked of longing to be hidden within the Five Wounds and the idea emerged in a prayer dating to the fourteenth century. This prayer became much loved by St Ignatius Loyola of the sixteenth century and it is called *Anima Chrisi* which means 'Soul of Christ':

> Soul of Christ, sanctify me
> Body of Christ, save me,
> Blood of Christ, inebriate me,
> Water from Christ's side, wash me,
> Passion of Christ, strengthen me,
> O Good Jesus, hear me.
> Within thy wounds hide me
> Suffer me not to be separate from thee.

The full and true meaning of the crosses on the heck posts in the North York Moors and Lancashire remained obscured, hidden and often misrepresented until now. Perhaps that is a long-term tribute to the wisdom, ingenuity and commitment of Father Postgate and his seventeenth century recusant congregations?

We shall never be sure that he left those crosses as a mark of his faith but we do know that he planted daffodils both at his Hermitage near Ugthorpe on the moors and elsewhere around the area of his tough mission. For those of a poetic or less militant nature,

Father Postgate's yellow daffodils are more gentle emblems of renewal and resurrection, blooming as they do at Easter with all their symbolism of new life.

Could four of their six petals be another form of the X-mark—a yellow one—with a large heart in the centre? Did he regard the humble daffodil as a potent emblem of the re-birth of his religion? In addition, according to local tradition in Egton Bridge, he also left the hymn he composed whilst in York Prison (chapter 13), and it will be noted it also contained a reference to the Wounds of Christ. In fact, he wrote of *seeing* those Wounds, perhaps an acknowledgement of their potent imagery.

Father Postgate may no longer be with us, but there are everlasting reminders of his faith and devotion in the daffodils that repeatedly bloom in and around the North York Moors. They, the crosses, the mighty 'Cathedral of the Moors' church in Egton Bridge and his hymn survive in that moorland area as inescapable reminders of modern English Catholicism in its second spring.

Notes

[1]   The contribution about the Five Wounds comes from Ajahn Punnyo, a senior Buddhist monk of the Therevada tradition in Thailand.

[2]   Dom Bede Camm, *Forgotten Shrines* (Leominster: Gracewing, 2004), p. 104.

[3]   William Wordsworth in his famous 'White Doe of Rylstone' re-wrote the story of the Nortons' role in this uprising.

[4]   G. W.Boddy, 'Players of Interludes in North Yorkshire in the early seventeenth century' in *North Yorkshire County Record Office Publication* N° 7, Journal 3(1976).

[5]   It is doubtful whether Simpson and Postgate attended the same classes at school, Postgate (13) being reported as several years younger than the senior Simpson (36) in 1616.

CHAPTER 9

A prelude to martyrdom

A S THE YEARS passed during Father Postgate's ministry of the moors, so the restrictions and penalties for being a Catholic, in particular a Catholic priest, were gradually eased and not strictly enforced. At national level a more understanding official attitude was being adopted and it is known that Father Postgate was generously assisted in his very localised work by many Protestants. Because they lived and worked on the moors, his activities were undertaken among them and beside them—they knew who and what he was, but they would offer food and shelter during his lonely treks. Furthermore, they did not inform the authorities about his work and whereabouts. In return, he helped them in any way possible. He would listen to their worries and concerns, give advice of a spiritual nature where necessary or offer practical help if that was required. He continued to share his gifts of food with those less fortunate than he. Another of his beloved acts was that if he found it necessary to impose a severe penance upon a penitent, he would offer to do half of it himself. If someone insulted or hurt him, he would explain his own short-coming to his assailant instead of criticising him. His actions indicate that he had a very deep understanding of human nature and he was able to make friends with total strangers. It is not surprising that, among those he knew well, many became converts to Catholicism or perhaps some who returned to that faith having earlier abandoned it.

Incidentally, the term 'Roman' Catholic did not appear until the early seventeenth century. It was a product of the Reformation and replaced several derogatory terms such as papism, papist, Romanism or Romanist.[1] It is now used with pride.

There is no doubt Father Postgate truly understood the psychology of the moorland people amongst whom he had been nurtured as a child and young man. In undertaking his mission upon the moors, he was in exactly the right place at the right time and it was he who managed to maintain the troublesome *bishopric of papists* at the forefront of national interest, and there is no doubt that, despite its small population and remote location, it became one of the strongest Catholic areas in England. A third of the population remained Catholic despite the persecution.[2]

Certainly the prevailing situation on those moors was not to the liking of the Protestant authorities but they tolerated it—in fact, they had little option. Over the years, they had tried repeatedly to stifle and outlaw the faith in and around Blackamoor but without success. Led by their charismatic missionary priest who was assisted by other priests recently returned to England from their training overseas, Father Postgate's patch of moorland became one of the most historic Catholic parishes in the country, not only during his time but for centuries afterwards.

If we consider the size of Blackamoor, we can appreciate the scale of his task but now that the purpose and distribution of the Mass posts has been revealed (for the first time) we can gain a better understanding of the breadth and scope of his activity. To my knowledge, his Mass Posts have been found in villages and dales around the moors, sometimes in very isolated places, but the biggest cluster was between Egton Bridge and Danby. They have also been recorded in Ainthorpe, Glaisdale, Beck Hole, Lealholm and Danby. That is not surprising—that part of Blackamoor was the main focus of his operations. However, the presence and location of those posts show that he travelled further afield—for example, there were Mass posts in Rosedale with others in Farndale,

Hutton-le-Hole, Gillamoor, Hawnby, Bilsdale and perhaps else-where.

At the other side of the moors there was a solitary one at Newton-on-Rawcliffe (upon his direct route between Egton and Pickering) and two near Scarborough, one being at Silpho and the other probably near Hackness. The latter is now in the Pitt Rivers Museum at Oxford where it is shown as coming from *'an unknown old house near Scarborough'* but nothing else is known of its history. All attempts to locate that unknown old house have failed. Its post has five scrolls whilst its neighbour at Silpho has two indistinct ones. The Silpho post bears signs of having had its X-mark removed, probably by local Methodists who considered it a pagan symbol. The fact that these two posts bear scrolls suggests there were others in the vicinity, but no record of them has been found.

Hackness is a lovely village close to the moors and there used to be a monastic establishment there. It is my suggestion that it is the most likely location of that puzzling post and another thought is that the presence of a Mass post in Hackness would probably be one of Father Postgate's cheeky reactions to the troublesome Hackness magistrate, the Puritanical Sir Posthumous Hoby.

Conversely, as mentioned in the previous chapter, none has been reported in or near Ugthorpe which was his home but we must accept they could have been removed. Similarly, there were no known Mass Posts in the East Riding, West Riding or the Kilving-ton area where Father Postgate first ministered. That was probably because he had the use of secret chapels in large houses. Secret signs that indicated other Mass centres were not therefore necessary. Rather curiously, however, I did come across a report of a Mass post in a house at Great Ouseburn not far from the Marston Moor, site of the famous battle in 1644. Until shortly before that time, Father Postgate had been the chaplain at Saxton Hall, so could he have occasionally left there to visit and celebrate Mass in the outlying area around Ouseburn?

One curiosity was that the house in question was called Gilling House—and a seat of the Fairfax family, long-time patrons of Father Postgate, was at Gilling Castle, near Helmsley. Of further interest is that the house dates to the seventeenth century and I spotted the necessary reference in a 'House for Sale' advert in the Yorkshire Evening Press of 3rd July 1993. A witch post was mentioned in the advert. However, when I tried to find out where the post had gone, the owner at the time (February 2008) had no knowledge of it or its whereabouts. So did Father Postgate celebrate Mass at Great Ouseburn, then in the West Riding of Yorkshire? Perhaps we shall never know.

However, we do know that he visited another place not far from his home on the moors. That is the market town of Pickering between Scarborough and Helmsley.

In his book *The North Riding of Yorkshire* (1906), Joseph Morris describes Pickering as 'An old-fashioned stone-built town on the southern verge of Blackamoor' which is still quite accurate and it is interesting that Mr Morris used the term 'Blackamoor' rather than The North York Moors. There is no doubt that Father Postgate walked the moors between Ugthorpe, Egton Bridge and Pickering, almost certainly using a direct route via two very remote and elevated hamlets, ie: Stape and Newton-on-Rawcliffe. A length of Roman road survives on that moorland.

Pickering is about twelve miles from Egton Bridge and Father Postgate could have covered that distance comfortably on foot within a day even when elderly. Even if he started his journey from The Hermitage some three miles or so further away, he could still complete his hike within a day. However, it seems he had a place of refuge *en route* where he could rest in safety and also celebrate Mass. It was Pond Cottage at Newton-on-Rawcliffe and we know that because the cottage, much altered from its original form, contains a Mass post.

This one, however, now stands away from the hearth simply because the fireplace area has been re-designed; the post itself has not been moved and it now supports the dining room roof. Interestingly it has no scrolls and that suggests the white-sheet system was not used here. The likelihood is it would not be necessary— even now there are few houses between Egton Bridge and Pickering via this route, and in Father Postgate's time there would be fewer. This Mass Centre was probably well known to Catholics and their priests as the only safe house on that very remote part of Blackamoor.

Pickering is a charming small town known today for its castle, its wonderful church of Saints Peter and Paul, the Beck Isle Museum, the terminus of the North York Moors Historic steam railway and the nearby Flamingo Park zoo. There is not the space in this modest volume to detail the town's extensive history, save to say that the castle dates from Norman times although much of its stonework is from the 14th century. The castle belongs to the Duchy of Lancaster and has many royal connections. Undoubtedly the most important building in Pickering from a Catholic point of view (apart from St Joseph's Catholic Church dating from 1911!) is the parish church of Saints Peter and Paul, now Anglican but with a long and interesting early Catholic history.

It contains one of the finest displays of medieval wall-paintings anywhere in Yorkshire or even in England. Dating from c.1450– 1460 and the work of an unknown artist, they depict biblical scenes that would have been used by priests and teachers to illustrate stories from the Bible at a time when most of the congregation was illiterate. As an aide to teaching, they would have been both magnificent and functional. The pictures, along with others in many more churches, were concealed beneath a coating of whitewash on the orders of Edward VI, the son of Henry VIII.

Although Henry had destroyed the monasteries and plundered them for their wealth, he continued to practice his Catholic faith, but died in January 1546/7. He was succeeded by his son, Edward VI, the first English monarch to be raised as a Protestant. He was nine years old when he succeeded to the throne.

The child king was ripe for manipulation by a strong Protestant faction of the Privy Council who suggested he embark on a 'Visitation' of his kingdom to ensure that all parish churches and their congregations had conformed to the official new religion. Edward agreed and so the kingdom was divided into six regions. Thirty commissioners were despatched to those regions ahead of the King's Visitation to make sure the churches were properly prepared for the Sovereign's arrival. All churches had to reflect his Protestant faith and the task of the commissioners was to make celebration of the old (Catholic) faith impossible. This was done by the simple process of removing everything the Catholics required or used during Mass and other church services. And so, upon orders from the nine year old Edward VI, the churches were ransacked and so began the wholesale destruction of anything that the authorities considered to be 'papist superstition.'

Altars were removed from the chancels, their altar stones smashed and any relics therein destroyed or dispersed. Rood screens were ripped out and any statutes they bore were torn away or burnt, holy water stoups were removed, candles taken away, other statutes were smashed, all wall paintings were covered up with lime-wash, and anything concerning the Virgin Mary was removed. Objects that may look like a relic, holy image, statue or religious picture were destroyed and in some cases even stained glass windows were smashed or removed for future sale. Processions and pilgrimages were banned.

In some parishes, however, the faithful learned of the impending arrival of the Commissioners and managed to remove and conceal some of the precious holy objects but in general the actions of the Commissioners were robust and thorough.

Pickering Church was one of those attacked including many local ones such as Kirkdale Minster, Kirkbymoorside and many others around the moors. Apart from the other indignities inflicted upon Pickering Church, those remarkable wall paintings were hidden beneath a coat of lime-wash and they remained concealed until they were accidentally discovered in 1853. One of my reference books published in 1874 records that they were again wilfully destroyed soon after discovery by a new coat of limewash.[3] That book adds that it is possible the second coat of lime-wash contained no size in which case the author felt the paintings might re-appear. That was a good forecast because they were re-discovered in 1880 when their full impact was revealed and today they can be seen by the public. It is said that Father Postgate wept when he saw the damage to Pickering church. He seems to have remained in Pickering for a few days at a time, making use of a cottage under the castle walls in a place that became known as Martyr's Field. The cottage had formerly belonged to a gardener who may have worked at the Castle and it was said to be situated along the Whitby road (not the present one) but my efforts to trace it were not successful.

With only two Catholics in Pickering when Father Postgate arrived, he was able to say Mass and accommodate his small congregation in his cottage but he announced Mass in the traditional way by hanging out white washing or sheets. But he did not require a Mass post in Pickering.

Of some interest to pilgrims visiting Pickering is the Bay Horse Inn in the market place because it has an inglenook fireplace in daily use complete with an extended heck post but no Mass post. Until around c.2007–9 there was a priests' hiding place in the stonework of the upper floor but it was lost when the upper rooms were upgraded. It is intriguing to think Father Postgate might have used that hiding place.

During the Civil War, Parliamentary troops were billeted at the old inn and within the castle but also in the church. It is widely suggested that the covering of lime-wash protected those paintings from the wrath of the Puritan soldiers who would have destroyed them as being offensive and superstitious.[4] So did the first efforts to obliterate the paintings in fact contribute to their long-time survival?

With regard to Father Postgate's love of gardening, it has long been the tradition that he pruned a pear tree that grew somewhere near his cottage in Pickering but my explorations and my questions from some of the local inhabitants, failed to identify either the pear tree or the cottage. Of further interest is Father Postgate's portable altar stone on the altar of St Joseph's Catholic Church at Potter Hill at Pickering. The amazing history of that stone is contained in Chapter 14.

We know very little about those years he spent trekking around Blackamoor in what he become his life-time's mission. There are stories about some of his remarkable escapes from pursuivants, stories of him coping with country folk who believed in witchcraft, stories of him planting daffodils with just a hint of mischief but no hint of any close friendships, true dramas and illnesses.

However apart from the Radcliffe family of Ugthorpe, he did have another friend, albeit perhaps not a very close one. Or it may be that this fellow claimed Father Postgate as a friend when he may have been little more than an acquaintance. His name was Thomas Ward, an author and poet who was born at Danby Castle and who lived there during Father Postgate's tenancy of The Hermitage.

The two dwellings were about seven miles apart, with both being on elevated sites with staggering views across the moors and dales. Thomas Ward was born in 1642 which made him some forty years

younger than Father Postgate. Born a Calvinist, he became a
Catholic and was author of several works that supported his new
faith. He was also widely travelled on the continent, visiting France,
Italy and Rome where, for six years, he served with the Papal Guard.
He claimed to know Father Postgate well, but returned to England
in 1685, six years after the priest's martyrdom then went back to
France where he died in 1708. His writings were considered very
revolutionary at the time, and he also wrote a poem entitled
'England's Reformation' that recounted the fate of those who
suffered in the aftermath of the Oates Plot.
One verse reads:

Nor spar'd they Father Postgate's blood,
A revered priest, devout and good,
Whose spotless life, in length was spun
To eighty years and three times one.
Sweet his behaviour, grave his speech,
He did by good example teach;
His love right bent, his will resign'd
Serene his look and calm his mind
His sanctity to that degree
As angels live, so lived he.

Apart from his literary activities we know very little of Thomas
Ward and how he came to be born and to live at Danby Castle
except that the castle appears to have been a ruin around the 15th
century.

Dating from the thirteenth century it was a seat of the Bruces,
the Latimers and the Nevilles but it seems that it was ruinous by
the seventeenth century where it was little more than a farmhouse
with the remains of a castle in the stackyard, as it is today. It may
be that Thomas Ward was not of noble birth but was a farmer's son.

However, I discovered a report of a Mass post in Danby Castle
but a search of the castle remains failed to reveal it. I believe it

formed part of the farmhouse which was occupied at my arrival, but neither the tenant nor the estate which owns the castle knew anything of the post and had never seen it. It is probably hidden somewhere in that farmhouse where it is being used as a lintel with its crosses concealed—it was said this post had two crosses rather like one at Postgate Farm, Glaisdale. It could be uncovered at some future time.

This lends strength to a theory that Father Postgate's mission took him to Danby where several houses had Mass Posts—one with a dozen scrolls—suggesting a busy Catholic area that probably extended into Farndale, Rosedale and Bilsdale. It might also explain why Father Postgate had cut an X-marked Mass post in Danby Castle—and it could also explain how and where he met Thomas Ward.

So let's take a closer look at Thomas Ward. If he was born in 1642, that was when Father Postgate was serving as chaplain to the Hungates at Saxton, in the West Riding of Yorkshire. In fact it was the year Lady Hungate died and Father Postgate moved to Halsham in the East Riding near Spurn Head.

From there, he served at Everingham and later at North and South Kilvington near Thirsk, returning to Blackamoor around 1662. Ward would be around 20 at that time. We do not know when he went across the Channel to France and Italy.

However, we do know he served five or six years in the Papal Guard and returned to England in 1685, six years after Father Postgate was martyred.[5] So how did he come to know Father Postgate?

If there is a Mass post hidden somewhere in Danby Castle, it could tell a story. If we imagine Father Postgate returning to Blackamoor c.1662 when Thomas was 20, then it is quite feasible the pair would meet when Father Postgate visited the farm at Danby Castle to say Mass with his Mass post prominently on show.

So how many white sheets would be put out in that case? We will not know until that post is discovered and we can count its scrolls.

On a personal note, as a child I used to play in the dungeon at Danby Castle; I think I might have been taken there by my grandfather who was a member of Danby Court Leet which met at the Castle. But I cannot recall ever seeing an X-marked post!

Notes

1   See *Brewer's Dictionary of Phrase and Fable* (London: Cassell and Co, 2000).
2   See British History Online (www.british-history.ac.uk), Parishes, Egton.
3   *Handbook for Travellers in Yorkshire* (London: John Murray, 1874).
4   Gordon Home, *The Evolution of an English Town* (Pickering: Blackthorn, 1905).
5   Elizabeth Hamilton, *The Priest of the Moors* (London: DLT, 1980).

CHAPTER 10

Trouble Ahead

A<small>S TIME PASSED</small>, Father Postgate could be forgiven for believing that the difficulties he had faced on a daily basis were drawing to a peaceful close. And as he grew older and wiser it became apparent that the Protestant authorities had become more tolerant of Catholics. Certainly on Blackamoor there were fewer prosecutions and not so many fines as Government agencies and their pursuivants relaxed their vigilance. The stage had almost been reached where Catholics could move in freedom without penalties, apprehension or ridicule, although caution was wise.

Despite the mood of tolerance, those productive years of Father Postgate's ministry were tough but happy. His work—and indeed his increasingly aged life—were almost over as more people were rejoining or being converted to the ancient English faith that was so much part of the worldwide communion. More baptisms were being conducted and more weddings celebrated. There were many funerals too but they were still carried out in secret so that the dear departed could go to their final resting places with the full benefit of a Catholic service. Even so, the actual burial, to conform to the civil law, had to be carried out in a Church of England graveyard with a burial service prescribed by the established church. This affected Methodists, Quakers, Baptists and other non-conformists as well as Catholics. As a consequence during the Penal Times, most Catholic burials were completed in secret with Requiem Mass. Some priests celebrated Requiem Mass ahead of the legally required Protestant service but in the case of Blackamoor it was said that each Catholic burial by Father Postgate had a daffodil bulb planted upon the grave. For some, however, their burials were completed in secret at night well away from the most popular areas. Protestants ignored this practice for they made no attempt to locate Catholic graves.

Those secret Catholic graves were never marked; families remembered where they were and could visit them. However, in 1880 the law was amended so that the dead could be buried without an Anglican Prayer Book Service. The necessary legislation received Royal Assent on 7th September 1880 and took immediate effect.

Following this, the very first funeral in England since the Reformation that was conducted according to the rites of the Catholic Church took place at Egton. The deceased was Maria Ripley, aged 16 of Egton Bridge. Egton Bridge had no graveyard of its own, but at Egton there was one graveyard for all denominations. That is where the present Mortuary Chapel now stands.

The parish priest, then Father Callebert, wrote formally to the vicar to inform him about the funeral, adding that he intended to read the Catholic funeral service over the grave that very day, adding, 'unless you can show me cause why I should not.' When the funeral procession reached the churchyard at Egton, the vicar was waiting and demanded to know by what authority Father Callebert was officiating. Father Callebert showed him a copy of the *York Herald* which announced the changes in the law with effect from 7th September—only six days earlier. The vicar responded by saying he had received no confirmation of the change from the Archbishop of York but he showed courage by bowing to Father Callebert and allowing him to go ahead. And so Maria Ripley and St Hedda's Church at Egton Bridge made history and her funeral went ahead with all the traditions of the Catholic Church.[1]

Long before that funeral, Father Postgate was still working as he approached (probably) eighty years of age, but the easing of relations between Catholics and Protestants was to be shattered. Trouble loomed again in London. Just when it seemed there would be a permanent relaxation in the persecution of Catholics, there was news of a serious crisis that involved the King and Parliament.

Violent attacks on Catholics and their properties followed a rapidly spreading rumour that a Catholic plot had been uncovered in London—and it was nothing less than a plot to murder King Charles II, take over the Government and the Navy and re-establish Catholicism as the national religion. Catholics were blamed again for the Fire of London in 1666, and the rumours revived memories of that dreadful time even though Catholics had been proved not responsible. The new rumours added that Protestants would be massacred in their thousands and the result was mass panic that spread like wildfire across England and deepened the hatred and mistrust of the Catholic population.

In June 1678, a man called Titus Oates and a fellow conspirator, Israel Tonge, DD, the Protestant Rector of St Michael's Church, Wood Street, London had collected what Oates described as a huge amount of written evidence that supported the intelligence that Catholics were scheming to assassinate King Charles II and take over the country by armed force. Oates conveyed this information to one of King Charles' confidential servants, a man called Christopher Kirkby, who in turn informed the King. However, Privy Councillors quickly realised the documents were false but in the meantime King Charles had summoned Titus Oates to a private interview. But after only a few minutes Charles realised Oates was a rogue and buffoon and dismissed him with the words, 'For my part, I call the man a lying knave.'

Both Charles and the Attorney General were positive the plot was completely false but instead of being angry at Oates' audacity, they were highly amused by the antics of this smelly, ugly and most unpleasant of men. They decided Oates was extremely stupid, particularly as he had tried to convince the King in person along with his Attorney General, and so they regarded this incident as little more than a humorous episode. But if Titus Oates was stupid, he was also cunning.

He did not give up. He went away and worked on his story, adding more 'facts' and 'statements from witnesses' to give it credence. Once he had strengthened his story, he approached Sir Edmund Berry Godfrey, the Justice of the Peace for Westminster, London. He told Sir Edmund that he wished to swear an affidavit that would confirm the dreadful truth of his allegations. That affidavit was sworn on oath on September 6, 1678. Once again, Oates found himself before the King, this time at the Privy Council where, for the second time, the King demolished his 'plot' theory with a few very well chosen questions.

Then Oates had a slice of devilish luck. He had named, as one of the 'plotters', a man called Coleman who was secretary to the Duchess of York and by chance, some letters were found in private papers belonging to Coleman. They were addressed to a French person and appeared to suggest the French should join forces with the English Catholics to overthrow the English Protestant regime.

Slender though this was as proof of a conspiracy, the letter was enough to give some credence to the stories told by Titus Oates. It was sufficient to re-ignite the powerful rumours of a Catholic plot to kill the King and overthrow Parliament. The rumours indicated the Pope was going to entrust the Government of England to the Jesuits, that they would appoint Catholics to all the highest posts in the land, that having burnt down London once, the Papists were going to do so again, that they were going to set fire to all the shipping in the River Thames, that Catholics would rise together at a given signal and assassinate all their Protestant neighbours, that the supportive French army would land in Ireland, that all leading statesmen and Protestant clergymen in England would be massacred, that various schemes had been drawn up to kill the King, either by stabbing, poisoning or shooting with a silver bullet—and so the country went berserk, seeing the devil in Catholics everywhere.

And it was entirely false.

Despite their absurdity, the rumours spread like rip-fire through London and then into the provinces; they spread faster and further than the flames of the Great Fire and as a consequence widespread panic and abject fear beleaguered the nation, these flames of fear being fanned by extremists even though there was no plot. The wholesale slaughter of Catholic priests and other Catholics began, making good use of the existing, but recently neglected Elizabethan legislation. When eventually the Oates plot was found to be false it was too late. The damage had been done. Ten Jesuit priests, five seminary priests, three Franciscan monks, two Benedictine monks and four Catholic laymen had been hanged for their alleged part in it. Catholics continued to be blamed for the Great Fire of London, for plotting to overthrow the King and his parliament and for any other misfortune that befell the country.

There was continuing mass hysteria with Catholics being hunted down and murdered or priests being declared traitors and found guilty of high treason to be formally hung, drawn and quartered for absolutely no reason other than their Catholic faith.

Then a fortnight or so after Oates had sworn his dreadful affidavit, Sir Edmund Berry Godfrey disappeared. On Saturday, 12th October 1678, he had failed to return home, consequently a search, organised by his man-servant John Reeves, was launched. It was known that Sir Edmund had been seen walking alone up St Martin's Lane when he had asked someone the way to Primrose Hill. He had also been seen in Marylebone before 1pm. He had not been seen since. Efforts by the search party had spread its tentacles across greater London but had failed to find him. All his usual haunts, friends and contacts were visited but no-one had seen the magistrate.

Then five days later, on Thursday, 17th October, his body was found about two and a half miles from the centre of London. It was discovered about 6pm by a farmer and a baker who chanced to be passing some waste ground on Primrose Hill. His body was face down and fully clothed with no evidence of a struggle, although many feet had trampled upon the scene and they would surely have ruined any evidence necessary to prove a person's guilt or to establish how the crime had been committed. Sir Edmund's wallet remained but his money had been stolen; his cravat and bands were also missing, whilst his periwig and hat were on a bush near the body. One of his gloves lay on a hedge. There was a superficial wound on his left shoulder and a vivid line around this throat, suggesting strangulation. His sword was also transfixing the body to the ground. Two boys who had been seeking a lost calf testified that the body had not been there on the Monday or Tuesday.

As the enquiries progressed, it became increasingly likely that he had been attacked and murdered elsewhere and his body dumped on Primrose Hill. The mark on his neck produced an unproven theory he had committed suicide by hanging and that friends or relations had cut down his body and taken it deep into the countryside in the hope he would not be recognised. They did not want his splendid reputation tainted by the suggestion he had taken his own life.

But if he *had* committed suicide, why would he have done so? There was no reason or evidence to suppose that was true. Those who knew him said Sir Edmund was not the sort of person who would take his own life.

But there was another mystery—although Sir Edmund's body had suffered that strange wound from his own sword, the lack of blood suggested it had happened after death. So was it someone exacting a revenge for past acts carried out by Sir Edmund?

Was he being blackmailed—there was a suggestion that his wealth had not been acquired by totally honest means and that he was on the fringes of the criminal world—certainly, he ranked known criminals among his friends. Many mysteries surrounded the life and death of Sir Edmund Berry Godfrey. A £500 reward—then a huge amount—was offered for information leading to his killers but it was never claimed in spite of three Catholics called Green, Berry and Hill being arrested on highly dubious evidence, and then executed. Subsequent investigations proved their innocence and so Sir Edmund's death remained—and still remains—a complete mystery.

Among those who fervently believed there had been a nation-wide plot by Catholics, even if the precise details were open to doubt, was Sir Edmund's manservant, John Reeves.

In his own personal deep-seated and long-standing hatred for members of that faith, he convinced himself they had murdered Sir Edmund Berry Godfrey, their motive being that he had accepted the affidavit from Titus Oates. That action had led to many Catholic deaths and, in Reeves' mind, they would have wanted to execute their revenge against the magistrate. That was their motive—in his mind. In convincing himself of their culpability, and for all their other wrongs, whether real or imagined, John Reeves wanted retribution.

He was something of a mystery man and it was claimed he had formerly served with HM Customs and Excise in Whitby where he had been a surveyor. His task had been to board ships before they docked to inspect their cargo and determine the level of duty the ship must pay. This mean he was also skilled in making enquiries, deal with the wrongdoers and formulating files that could be used in evidence in a court of law.

His time with HM Customs at Whitby meant he would have known Egton's role as a hot-bed of papists led by a charismatic local priest. And suppose those papists were plotting to store arms and explosives in readiness for their attack on King and Country?

John Reeves decided to target the Catholics, this time in Whitby and upon the surrounding moors and he would make good use of the intelligence already gathered about the papist bishopric of that remote region. In the troubled mind of John Reeves that was the ideal place to catch a Catholic, preferably a priest, and make him an example to the nation.

We cannot be absolutely sure why John Reeves decided to trek to Whitby to wreak his revenge but he did so and there were those who thought Reeves was truly Sir Edmund's murderer and that he had fled to Yorkshire to evade detection.

But John Reeves had a highly important task ahead. As a matter of record, the murder of Sir Edmund Berry Godfrey has never been solved but John Reeves said he was going avenge the death of his master by catching a Catholic priest.

Notes

[1]   See John Dunleavy, '"This long-standing, vexed question":—the burial of non-Anglicans in parish churchyards' in *Northern Catholic History* 51(2010), pp. 10–14.

CHAPTER 11

The arrest

ERY LITTLE IS known about John Reeves. We do not have any personal details of his life. We do not know his age, whether he was married or had a family, his employment prior to becoming the manservant of Sir Edmund Berry Godfrey or details of his previous work, probably at Whitby, as an officer in HM Customs and Excise. What is known, however, is that, following the murder of his master, Reeves left London with the sole intention of arresting Father Nicholas Postgate, the renowned Catholic priest whose exploits and successes at keeping the old faith alive on Blackamoor was known at the highest level within Parliament.

It is extremely likely that Reeves went first to Whitby to renew his acquaintance with the current staff of the Customs House. The man in charge was Allan Wharton who had been appointed His Majesty's Collector of Customs for the Crown, a new and important post in Whitby. He was the first holder of that office, having been appointed in 1671. Reeves' purpose was to announce his presence in the area but specifically to seek help from other established law enforcement officers, all of whom would be known to Allan Wharton even if they operated inland. Certainly, teams of Customs Officers operated inland; they worked on horseback and were known as Riding Officers, their duties being to look out for smugglers and other illegal operators whose activities took them deep into Blackamoor and beyond.

Reeves also knew that through a law recently approved by King Charles II (13 & 14 Car.2, c.12, s.15) the responsibility for the appointment of constables, hitherto the privilege of the Lord of the Manor, had now passed to local magistrates.

Because Yorkshire's Eskdale—the part of Blackamoor that interested Reeves—was under the jurisdiction of Whitby Strand magistrates, two of those magistrates would be required to jointly appoint parish constables for one year at a time. At the end of every year, each constable would be discharged from his duties or perhaps re-appointed. Once appointed, however, the constables were responsible to the magistrates for the maintenance of law and order and the preservation of the King's Peace within their area of responsibility. Their wages would be paid by the Church of England through their parish funds, and whenever necessary they would be assisted by churchwardens. One administrative and very practical problem was that with such a short period of commitment, the constables regularly changed and it was difficult keeping track of them and their whereabouts, or to establish any kind of continuity of local knowledge.

Reeves quickly learned that one of the Whitby mariners, Henry Cockerill, was a part-time conservator of the peace and he had a cousin called William Cockerill who was the constable responsible for a large district around Littlebeck and Ugglebarnby, duties he conducted in his spare time. That area was in the lower reaches of Eskdale and only five miles or so from Egton's Kirkdale, the infamous *bishopric of papists* that so worried Parliament. Responsible for the neighbouring district of Eskdale further up the valley of the River Esk—Egton and Glaisdale for example—was a constable called Robert Langdale who owned a fulling mill at Glaisdale. These men were to find themselves assisting John Reeves in his hunt for Father Postgate.

Reeves, always most professional, was acutely aware that, in recent times, Father Postgate had been allowed to travel and preach his religion virtually unchallenged throughout the moors and villages of Blackamoor.

Sometimes quite openly he celebrated Mass, baptised children, conducted weddings and funerals, all within what was officially the forbidden religion. It was known that local Protestants would protect Father Postgate too. Through the latter years of his ministry, therefore, not one of the local officials had seen fit to challenge him or to bring him to justice. Even at Parliamentary level there had been a softening of attitude towards Catholics, although that was unofficial and the Penal Laws remained in force. However, due to the activities of John Reeves that state of affairs was about to change.

Before speaking to his future colleagues, he decided that if he formulated an operation to trap the priest actually in the act of celebrating Mass or, for example, conducting some other Catholic sacrament such as baptising a child or officiating at a wedding, he would probably meet resistance accompanied by a veil of secrecy. After all, the old priest—now about 80 years of age - had been allowed to continue his activities unchallenged so Reeves realised his task was not going to be easy. But, he argued with himself, the law remained on his side.

He decided that he would gather his men together for their first briefing when he would outline the impact of the Papist Plot in London, stressing that some of the information provided by Titus Oates and Israel Tonge had been true, and that a massive Papist uprising had been planned from Yorkshire where arms and ammunition had been stored in secret for later use by the Catholic traitors to whom Oates had referred. Reeves, described as an 'implacable enemy of Catholicks as the supposed murtherers of his master'[1] would tell his assistants that if the plan had gone ahead the King would have been killed, Parliament would have been taken over by the Papists and all resistance would have been halted by a show of arms and use of ammunition that had been steadily amassed over recent years.

And, continued Reeves, the leader was none other than Father Nicholas Postgate. He would inform those ill-informed country constables that Government spies had always been active in this region and it was they who had uncovered this Yorkshire branch of the infamous plot. He would claim that Nicholas Postgate was in fact a cunning and dangerous terrorist whose activities involved the recruitment of hundreds or even thousands of rebellious activists, plus the gathering and storage of arms and ammunition. Any raid Reeves conducted, therefore, would, (so he would inform his team), be to search for arms and ammunition that had been gathered and stored by the conspirators and not particularly for a priest who was merely celebrating Mass or the sacraments.

It is distinctly possible that he disguised his true purpose and intentions for being in the area, one theory being that his cover story stated he was surveying disused iron-ore mines because it was Parliament's intention to re-open any mines that were still viable. That ploy would allow Reeves to visit obscure locations and talk to local people in his intelligence-gathering exercises, with never a hint he was really hunting Father Postgate.

As he groomed his assistants into believing his story, he claimed that his years as a Customs Officer had taught him how to search for contraband and so he would lead any search in which his team was involved. And so, as John Reeves began to gather his own information and snippets of local gossip, he had a stroke of what for him was good fortune. He had attended a wedding somewhere in Eskdale when he overheard a farmer called Matthew Lyth say, 'You talk of papists and protestants, but when the roast is cut, I know who will have the first cut.'[2]

Reeves interpreted this as a sinister statement and his views were reinforced when William Cockerill, his companion and one of the local constables, also claimed to have heard Lyth utter a treacherous or subversive phrase whilst visiting Cockerill's house. He had said, 'A sorrowful Christmas, a bloody fastness (Shrove Tuesday), a joyful Easter.'[3] At this time, Christmas was only a few weeks away. Reeves explained to Cockerill that these suspicious words were those of a 'papist malcontent' and he then said that he would *'seek out the wretch and see if some armes and ammunition'* were stored on his premises.[4] Not only would Reeves accomplish his aim, he would also be paid the standard reward of £20 for the arrest of a papist traitor priest.

Whilst planning an opportunity to carry out the raid, Cockerill had learned that a child had been born at the Lyth household which was a farm known as Red Barns or Red Barn Farm, and that there were plans to have him baptised by none other than Father Nicholas Postgate. Red Barns stands today on the high road between Ugglebarnby and Littlebeck above Sleights some seven miles east of Egton and it overlooks Eskdale from the south. Coincidentally, Red Barns is only half a mile or so from Dean Hall which was thought by Hugh Aveling to be the birthplace of Father Nicholas Postgate. Certainly a Postgate family once lived at Dean Hall and were probably related to the Blessed Nicholas (see chapter 1).

It had taken several weeks for Reeves to locate this house and to be within reach of arresting a priest—the birth and subsequent baptism of a child was a wonderful bonus. Sir Edmund had been found dead on 17th October 1678 and the baptism was planned at Red Barns for 8th December, 1678, a Sunday.

That meant the priest would also be celebrating Mass and so Reeves would have to ensure his raid was professionally carried out so that he could seize any evidence of Postgate's priesthood in addition to anything that might be found during the baptismal ceremony. And then, of course, he and his men would have to thoroughly search the entire farm premises for hidden arms and ammunition. Indeed, reasoned Reeves, the officials would have to be armed too—one never knew how the subjects of such a raid would respond, even if women and children were present.

Another factor to bear in mind was that the house would have been made secure during the ceremony just in case a raid occurred—even though, in recent months, such raids had not been as common as in previous years, they were now increasing due to the spread of alarm from London after the actions of Titus Oates. With that in mind, the occupants of the various mass centres would lock their doors and private guards would be on duty. That would also apply to Red Barns during the Mass and baptismal ceremony.

Gaining entry to such a house especially with a priest in attendance and actually celebrating Mass would not be easy. No doubt windows and doors would be secure, there would be a plan to conceal any evidence of the Mass should a raid occur, and guards would be on duty, perhaps concealed around the premises, to raise the alarm if anything untoward seemed to be happening. But, in the mind of John Reeves careful planning and professionalism would ensure success. He set to work. One advantage was that if the Mass was held early in the morning, as was the custom, then, at that time of year, it would be dark outside the house whilst inside there would be candles and fires to light the interior. He would not be surprised if a decoy light was placed in the barn whereas the ceremonies might be inside the living area.

There would be tricks and ploys to prevent or frustrate the raid but Reeves felt that he, with all his skill and wide experience would have the advantage over these simple Yorkshire farmers. But the people of those moors also had a few tricks up their sleeves. Stories are told of them placing lights in their outbuildings and barns to mislead raiders before they realised their error—and their unwelcome presence would be announced by the noise of strategically placed geese and/or dogs. But such distractions gave occupants time to conceal any priestly possessions or altar furnishings. Another ploy was to install a bell in the through-passage that existed in most farms. As the raiders entered by either of the two doors, one at each end of the passage, the act of opening a door would ring a bell. The door that led into the living quarters—known as the firehouse—would be sturdy and locked. By the time the raiders had persuaded the occupants to open that inner door, all evidence of the Mass would have been concealed. This might include candles, a missal, priestly garments, a portable altar stone, a chalice and other essentials—including the priest. Another bonus was a house with lots of doors that provided escape routes—a safe-house required at least two doors, although Bridgeholme Green at Egton Bridge, in the heart of Father Postgate's Blackamoor had seven doors.

The attendance of several people in the house could be explained as a birthday party or a family gathering of some kind whilst a white-clothed table (used as a make-shift altar) would be laden with food to confirm that story. And large table-cloths reaching down to the floor could conceal a lot, as could long curtains. In some larger houses there may even be escape routes for the priests and probably in some larger houses there would be especially constructed hiding places for priests. For the occupants of a house that was liable to be raided, therefore, a range of delaying tactics were essential—vital time was required if the evidence was to be concealed.

We do not know what kind of protection was given to Red Barns just before the raid by John Reeves and Henry Cockerill. Furthermore, we do not know if they gained entry by force or coercion. Perhaps the Lyth family had been lulled into a false sense of security by the lack of activity during recent months and, of course, living

as they did in a remote part of the North York Moors, they may not
have heard about the frenzy in London and other parts of the
country that had resulted from the false claims of Titus Oates. To
provide a flavour of that time, the CTS Pamphlet *Ven. Nicholas
Postgate* quotes from Bede Camm's famous *Forgotten Shrines*:

> Besides the immediate victims of the infamous informers,
> Oates, Bedloe and their crew, priests were at that period
> hunted out and done to death all over the country; not
> indeed that they were included of having any share in the
> pretended plot, but merely for their faith and priesthood.
> Thus at Cardiff, Ruthin, Worcester, Hereford, York and
> other places, innocent servants of God were put to death
> amid scenes of atrocious ferocity for the sole offence that,
> having been ordained priests by the authority of the Holy
> See, they had dared to return to their country and remain
> in it for more than forty days in order to minister to souls.[5]

However, the outcome of Reeves' determined intention was successful. By means fair or foul, he and Henry Cockerill gained access
to Red Barns. We are not informed about their precise method of
entry but it seems the Lyth family and their friends, including
Father Postgate, had found themselves surprised by this turn of
events. Reeves and Cockerill had discovered a veritable gold mine.
They found a noted priest and three suspect laymen—Matthew
Lyth and friends called Luke Readman and Edmund Roe, plus
several items that formed part of Catholic worship, the Mass in
particular.

They did not find any arms or ammunition but did recover
several pieces of evidence that a Catholic religious service was being
held there, including 'popish books, relicks and wafers, and severall
other things'.[6]

Father Postgate was questioned at the scene by John Reeves who
asked the purpose of the various recovered items. The priest

answered that he 'disposed of them among several persons who desired them for their infirmities'[7] and under further questioning stated he had been given the items by a Mr Thomas Goodricke and a Mr John Jowsie. Both these gentlemen were priests who had been educated at the English College in Douai and who had helped Father Postgate during his mission on the moors, but both had died by this time. The prefix 'Mr' was often used for a priest at that time, the term 'Father' being of later origin.

When asked formally for his name, Father Postgate said it was Watson. There is little doubt that John Reeves found these answers rather evasive but we must remember that one of the practices of a priest caught in such circumstances was to protect the people around him. They were open, at the very least, to a charge of harbouring a priest.

When Father Postgate's cause was first opened at Westminster in 1923–26 with the evidence being later examined in Rome during 1929, the Devil's Advocate (now the Promoter General of the Faith) suggested that Father Postgate may not have shown perfect faith because he had hesitated in some of his answers to Reeves. Indeed, he did not admit he was a priest, saying instead 'Let them prove it' and this might have been interpreted as a weakness even though, in English law, a person is innocent until proven guilty. However the indications of possible sainthood did not concern John Reeves.

In his opinion, the evidence he had found was sufficient to justify the arrest of Father Nicholas Postgate, Matthew Lyth and the two other friends, Readman and Roe. They were transported to Brompton Hall near Scarborough, the home of Sir William Cayley who was the local Justice of the Peace. His son, William, a magistrate too, also lived at this house.[8]

But in Father Postgate's time, Sir William and his son had no thoughts about inventing aircraft. Their task was to examine the evidence of the charges against Father Postgate and his colleagues. In his role as Examining Magistrate, Sir William would have to decide whether there was sufficient evidence to commit Father Postgate and others to trial by jury at a forthcoming Assize Court in The Guildhall at York.

Notes

1   Elizabeth Hamilton, *The Priest of the Moors* (London: DLT, 1980, p. 57.

2   *Ibid.*

3   *Ibid.*

4   *Ibid.*, p. 58.

5   Father William Storey, *Ven. Nicholas Postgate* (London: Catholic Truth Society: 1928), p. 14. See also Dom Bede Camm, *Forgotten Shrines* (Leominster: Gracewing, 2004).

6   Hamilton, *The Priest of the Moors*, p. 58.

7   *Ibid.*

8   The later Cayley family became widely known through the inventive brain of Sir George Cayley. As early as 1804—ninety-nine years before the Wright Brothers' sustained flight by a man-carrying aircraft—Sir George experimented with a type of glider and by 1809 had produced one large enough to lift off the ground anyone who clung to it in flight. He then produced a tension wheel for his gliders to land upon and this was developed into the spoked bicycle wheel. Sir George also suggested the famous Sea Cut that prevents the River Derwent flooding around Malton and Pickering. By 1849, he had developed a machine with fixed wings, a three-wheeled undercarriage and adjustable controls that carried a boy aged 10 off the ground for several yards, then in 1853 he persuaded his coachman to sit upon an early aircraft which flew about fifty yards from side of Brompton Dale to the other. The coachman promptly resigned, saying 'I wish to give notice. I was hired to drive, not to fly'—and this was 51 years before the Wright Brothers fitted an engine to their aircraft.

CHAPTER 12

On trial

THERE ARE FOUR Bromptons in North Yorkshire—Brompton-on-Swale is between Richmond and Catterick whilst Patrick Brompton is between Bedale and Leyburn. These are close to the Yorkshire Dales. Another Brompton, sometimes known as Brompton-in-Allertonshire, lies close to Northallerton in the broad Vale of York, then Brompton-by-Sawdon is between Pickering and Scarborough just outside the southern boundaries of the North York Moors National Park.

Brompton-by-Sawdon is the seat of the Cayley family who originated in Norfolk and it was Edward Cayley who bought the estate at Brompton in the early seventeenth century. He fathered the Sir William Cayley who was a magistrate and eventual Mayor of Scarborough (in 1686) and it was he who heard the committal proceedings against Father Postgate. Brompton-by-Sawdon has several claims to fame apart from its links with aviation history (see Chapter 11)—it was the scene of the marriage in 1802 between the poet William Wordsworth and Mary Hutchinson. Mary was from Gallows Hill Farm nearby and they married in the Brompton's Church of All Saints that dates from the thirteenth century or possibly earlier in Saxon times. Once containing a shrine to Our Lady in its Catholic days, it would be standing in its damaged and reformed style when Father Postgate was escorted to Brompton Hall along with Matthew Lyth, Luke Readman and Edmund Roe. However, the present Brompton Hall dates only from the late 18th century and it appears to have been built by the Cayley family to replace an older manor house. That more recent house is now a residential school.

Father Postgate would have been taken to that older house because it fulfilled the role of a magistrates' court and it also had a least one detention cell or lock-up.

In fact, if it was to accommodate Father Postgate and his three colleagues, there would have been more cells but it is not certain how long these men remained at Brompton Hall. These legal proceedings were not a trial. It was not the purpose of this court to determine innocence or guilt. The hearing was known as Committal Proceedings during which the magistrates had to consider the evidence and if necessary call witnesses to determine whether or not there was a case to answer at a higher court. If the magistrates felt there was not sufficient evidence to justify such a trial, the prisoners would be released without further charge. If they decided the evidence *was* sufficient to justify a trial, they would be remanded in custody until the next Assizes.

During that preliminary hearing, the magistrates took down written statements known as depositions and it was these that formed the basis for a future trial, if any.

That preliminary hearing took place on 9th December 1678, the day following Father Postgate's arrest, when Sir William Cayley and his son took sworn depositions from Father Postgate, John Reeves, William Cockerill, Henry Cockerill and Robert Langdale. Apart from Father Postgate's own testimony, all the other witnesses acted for the prosecution. There was no system for defending an accused person at that time—his or her fate depended upon the jury. In this instance, it seemed that the magistrates were not entirely confident about the evidence supplied by the witnesses. Much of it was circumstantial without any direct proof of Father Postgate's priesthood—certainly it was true that popish articles and books had been found when he was arrested but other people who were not priests were known to possess such objects. Possession of a Catholic Mass book did not make its owner a priest.

For example, Elizabeth Hamilton in her book *The Priest of the Moors* provided an account of the evidence of William Cockerill who said that 'he had often seen the person now apprehended, known by the name of Postgate, going about the country; that he was generally believed to be, and was spoken of as, a popish priest.' Robert Langdale's evidence was not much better for he testified, 'he had heard of the prisoner Posket and that for many years he had been generally accounted a popish priest.'

It seems that the court authorities in York demanded more real evidence that was not hearsay. They required evidence from witnesses who had actually seen Father Postgate celebrating Mass or conducting any of his priestly duties. The task of finding those witnesses rested upon John Reeves in his role as prosecutor, and it appears he returned to the Whitby district and managed to trace some. They were examined some months after the first hearing, namely between 6th and 11th March, 1678, shortly before Father Postgate was arraigned at York Assizes. One of them was Elizabeth Baxter, a spinster aged about thirty who had been befriended by Nicholas Postgate and whom he had helped on many occasions. At the time of her depositions, Father Postgate was already in prison at York Castle awaiting his trial but she stated she had often seen the reputed priest and had heard him say Mass several times at the home of John Hodgson at Biggin House near Ugthorpe. Some eight or nine years previously he had given Holy Communion to her but afterwards she had abandoned the Catholic faith to become a Protestant and attended Anglican services. She had since moved from the Blackamoor area to live in Scarborough. Father Postgate is said to have been moved to tears by her evidence but some regarded this as a weakening of his faith. Elizabeth later visited him in prison to seek his forgiveness which he freely gave, along with some cash to enable her to return home.

Another witness was Elizabeth Wood, the wife of a man called RalphWood who was a mariner at Whitby. She testified she had known Father Postgate for ten or twelve years and had heard him say Mass at the home of Thomas Pattison in Ugthorpe and at Timothy Lyth's house near Grosmont Bridge. She also added she had received Holy Communion from Father Postgate some seven or eight year earlier, and had seen others do the same. She had been a Protestant for the last six years.

The third witness was Richard Morrice, a much detested man known as Hang Priest Morrice. It seems he spent much of his time trying to get priests arrested. He swore he knew 'Mr Poskitt,' the popish priest, and had been married by him. He had also received Holy Communion from Father Postgate and had seen him give Communion to others; he added he had also seen Father Postgate celebrate Mass. Morrice had become a Protestant about twelve years earlier and constantly attended church. The evidence of these witnesses was sufficient for a trial to proceed but Nicholas Postgate was not to be charged with any offence or involvement connected with the Titus Oates plot and no charges were brought for any alleged storage of arms and ammunition.

The evidence was sufficient to confirm that Nicholas Postgate was a Catholic priest. It was deemed High Treason if a man was ordained a Catholic priest overseas and remained in England for more than forty days. There were many more ingredients to the Act, too many to summarise here. The infamous statute had been signed by Queen Elizabeth I in person and was *27. Elizabeth. Cap. 2*. It was entitled *An Act Against Jesuits and Seminarists* and was dated 1585. The penalty for High Treason was to be hanged, drawn and quartered and anyone convicted of assisting a priest would be treated as a felon and hanged.

Father Postgate was held prisoner in York Castle until his appearance at the next Lent Assizes, sometimes known as the Spring Assizes. Accompanying him were Matthew Lyth, Luke Readman and Edmund Roe. Apart from caring for his colleagues who found imprisonment most difficult to tolerate, there is no doubt Father Postgate made himself useful in prison and one of his achievements was to compose a hymn which has been sung at Egton Bridge and elsewhere since the day he was executed more than 330 years ago. I last heard it in July 2011 at the annual Postgate Rally at St Hedda's Church in Egton Bridge and it is regularly sung at funerals. Its opening line is 'O Gracious God, O Saviour Sweet' and although there is no direct evidence that he was the hymn's composer, it does include a verse that reads:

Behold dear Lord, I come to thee
With sorrow and with shame
For when Thy bitter wounds I see,
I know I caused the same.

My own view is that the reference to the Wounds of Christ, and bearing in mind Father Postgate's open devotion to the famous Five Wounds, persuades me that he is the hymn's composer.[1]

Unlike the murderers, robbers and rapists, he was not strictly confined to his cell and was allowed to visit other areas such as the kitchens, wash house and exercise yard. That implied he was a trusted person. In addition as a priest, he had been allowed to retain his portable Mass kit and so he said Mass daily in his cell, and in the cells of others who requested it. It wasn't long before he built up a small but enthusiastic prison congregation, with the warders ignoring this development. In their view it provided the prisoners with an additional activity which in turn kept them happier and occupied.

With regular meals and the shelter of his cell, Father Postgate did not find it at all arduous. Instead of ministering to the people of the moors, he found himself ministering to inmates and to some of their visitors. He realised that the Word of God must be made available to all prisoners and did his utmost to provide it at York in his own inimitable way.

There is no doubt that the yeoman farmers Readman, Roe and Lyth found it increasingly stressful to live in such conditions, and in such close proximity to other people. Accustomed to the open air and extensive space of their fields, woodlands and rivers, and to the demands of their livestock, they experienced immense difficulty in settling down to the confines of prison routine. All were young, healthy and strong, well able to defend themselves against any inmates who might be tempted to attack them or rob them of their food or modest possessions brought as gifts. The fact that all three were friends and always seen together was another bonus in their favour—few would risk attacking such a formidable group of strong young men. Only a fool would attempt that.

All of them, including Father Postgate, received regular visitors including family and friends. The priest found it gratifying that so many friends from his past—and their descendants - came to visit him in York. Among them were the Hungates from Saxton near Tadcaster in the West Riding with whom he had experienced his first missionary role upon his return from Douai in 1630; the Vavasours of Hazlewood Castle near Tadcaster, the Constables from Halsham and Burton Constable in the East Riding, the Meynells from Kilvington near Thirsk in the North Riding, the Fairfaxes at York and Gilling East near Helmsley. They came from other districts where he had served, perhaps only very briefly either as a travelling priest or at large country houses in his disguise as gardener, some perhaps being unknown.

Visitors also came from places as remote as Ugthorpe, Grosmont, Sleights, Egton, Egton Bridge, Beckhole, Glaisdale, Lealholm, Danby, Bilsdale, Farndale, Rosedale, Silpho, Hackness and the areas around Helmsley, Pickering, Whitby and Guisborough.

Unlike his first mission in Yorkshire where he had served the gentry and aristocracy between 1630 and c.1662–5 the people from the moors were ordinary men and women, some being yeomen, others craftsmen or mere labourers but all loved him and wanted him to know they cared about his future. A surprisingly large number were Protestants who had come to offer their condolences and who brought gifts of food and clothing, not only for him but for others in desperate need. Without exception, all his visitors asked for a priestly blessing that he freely gave.

The Assizes were scheduled to take place during the week from Monday 10th March until Saturday 15th March 1679 at the Guildhall, York. The fine building stood—and still stands - on the banks of the Ouse close to the Mansion House, and is a ten minute walk from the Castle. It was to this place that John Reeves was summoned as the prosecutor of Nicholas Postgate, Matthew Lyth, Luke Readman and Edmund Roe. They would not be summonsed —they would be escorted from the Castle to the Guildhall in a horse-drawn cart under armed guard. The witnesses Elizabeth Baxter, Elizabeth Wood and Richard Morrice were also summonsed, along with the two Cockerills and Robert Langdale. All were instructed to attend on the first day and to make themselves available on the premises until their case was heard. No day or time could be given—it would depend upon the progress of cases ahead of them in the calendar. The Assize court was open to the public whilst in session and so friends and relations could attend if they so desired, to sit in the public gallery.

For the ancient City of York, the arrival of the Assizes provided a reason for festivities, fairs and celebrations of every kind. Bunting was placed above the streets, flags were hoisted on buildings and churches, houses were decorated, music and dancing was encouraged in the parks and open spaces with displays by horsemen, archers, actors, jousters, jesters and clowns. The famous Knavesmire on the southern outskirts of York was the scene of many judicial hangings and other executions but it also staged fairs with horse races, food, drink, music, singing and dancing all within sight of the gallows, while the boats on the river were adorned with flags and lanterns which gleamed in the water at night.

It might be said that these amusements were for the ordinary people of York along with visitors who travelled into the city for this exciting experience. But it was not just for ordinary folk. For the aristocracy, landed gentry and businessmen of Yorkshire, the Assizes presented an opportunity for the wealthy and important to gather for social engagements and dinners with an opportunity to conduct important business deals. To act as host to the red Judge of Assize was considered one of the highest marks of achievement. Many people travelled in from the country homes and estates to their city houses merely to be present during the Assizes, and to make the most of opportunities presented by such a splendid gathering.

The gracious town mansions were aglow with lights and filled with laughter and music as socialites made use of York's more splendid assets. The atmosphere was one of gaiety and happiness. Then there was York's renowned civic pageantry, second only to London with its Lord Mayor, Sheriff, judges and other court officials processing in their regalia from the Judges' Lodgings to the Guildhall.

For the prisoners held in the Castle, however, it was a different story, a time of seemingly endless waiting and wondering with no-one to act in their defence. Father Postgate did not have long to wait. Because his trial was for the crime of high treason, it ranked as one of the most serious of charges, far more serious that either murder or robbery, and it was therefore scheduled early in the calendar. He was taken from his cell, placed in a cart and driven to the Guildhall flanked by two armed guards. He was placed in a dark cell beneath the courtroom and told to await his name being called. Because the alleged crimes of Readman, Roe and Lyth were of a lesser degree, they would be dealt with later in the week.

When his name was called, Father Postgate climbed the circular stone staircase that led into the courtroom, opening directly into the bar with its spiked rails. He stood and gazed at the court, noticing the crowded public gallery and the officials standing or sitting in their pre-determined places. Twelve jurors, all men, were sitting in the jury box too, staring at him with undisguised curiosity. He was probably the oldest and meekest defendant they were likely to encounter. At this point, the judge's chair was empty as was that of the sheriff. Soon a scarlet robed and bewigged judge appeared from the robing room and strode to his seat, followed by the sheriff in his formal attire. When everyone was settled, the judge looked at Father Postgate. Let us now imagine what followed.

'Is your name Nicholas Postgate?'

'It is, Your Honour.'

'And you are aged eighty years or thereabouts?'

'Yes, Your Honour.'

'And you are from a place popularly known as The Hermitage on the moors between Ugthorpe and Egton in the Wapentake of Langbargh East?'

'I am, Your Honour.'

The judge now turned his attention to the jury. 'Members of the jury, have you appointed a chairman from amongst your number?'

'Yes, Your Honour,' and a man in the front row of the jury box raised his hand. 'Name of Reuben Newton.'

'Good. Now listen carefully, members of the jury. The accused is charged with the treasonable crime of being a Catholic priest in contravention of the statute of 1585 known as 27 Elizabeth 1.2. That statute is almost a hundred years old, but still valid.'

The jury members nodded their acceptance of this knowledge. The judge continued,

'When the allegation was first put to the defendant at the commit-tal hearing, his reply was "Let them prove it." Does that remain your response, Mr Postgate?'

'It does,' replied the priest, quickly adding, 'Now, can I ask a question?'

'It is somewhat irregular, but yes. Go ahead.'

'Are there any Catholics on the jury, Your Honour?'

'Are you saying you wish to challenge the jury, Mr Postgate?'

'I just wish to ensure I receive a fair trial.'

'Then I can assure you of that. You will receive a fair trial, each of these jury members is fully qualified as laid down by statute. That is all that is necessary, their religion is not relevant. And, for the benefit of Mr Postgate, I shall remind the jury and the court of a recent case, dating from as recently as 1670, in which Mr Bushell established that the jury shall reach their verdict on the facts alone, and not upon any direction from the judge, or from any political interference or motivation. Does that satisfy you, Mr Postgate?'

'Yes, Your Honour.'

'Good, then let us proceed. Call the first witness, a Mr John Reeves who is an agent of the Government.'

And so Reeves, followed in turn by the two Cockerills and Robert Langdale appeared before the judge who read from the depositions they had provided before Sir William Cayley, asking if this was the evidence presented by them at that committal hearing. They agreed that it was. He then asked if the words written down were true, and whether they had in fact stated them on oath. All agreed that was the case and that their testimonies were true. The judge asked one or two simple questions, chiefly concerning the times and locations of Postgate's alleged crimes.

Satisfied with each official, he then dismissed them. Now it was the turn of the three witnesses. First was Elizabeth Baxter who was clearly very nervous, and who dared not to look at Father Postgate.

'Is your name Elizabeth Baxter?'

'Yes, Your Honour,' she replied softly.

'Speak up, woman!' snapped the judge. 'Everyone in this court must be able to hear you. Now, you are a spinster and you live in Scarborough?'

'Yes, Your Honour. But I used to live in Eskdale until the last two months or so.'

'Ah, that has answered my next question. So, Miss Baxter, do you recognise the prisoner?'

'Yes, I do, he is the priest, Mr Postgate.'

'A priest, you say?'

She realised she had made a simple error and lowered her head but the judge continued,

'Miss Baxter. You made a very comprehensive and clear deposition before Sir William Cayley, do you stand by the evidence you presented at his examination, evidence that was given on oath?'

'Yes, Your Honour, I do.'

'Then let me remind you of what you said; members of the jury, listen carefully to every word. Mr John Reeves, the prosecutor, will read out each deposition.'

And so he took Elizabeth, and then Elizabeth Wood and finally Richard Morrice through their individual statements, reciting the words so the jury could hear them. Each stated they had seen Father Postgate saying Mass or carrying out other priestly functions. After each deposition had been read aloud, the witnesses were asked questions by the judge about various facts, dates, time and places, always directing the jury to listen carefully. During Elizabeth Baxter's testimony, however, after stating she had witnessed Father Postgate saying Mass at Biggin House, Ugthorpe, the old priest was moved to tears and many years later, when Father Postgate's Cause was heard in Rome and he was declared Venerable, those tears were interpreted as a weakening of his faith. But in truth, the tears were *for* Elizabeth—and later she came to him to seek forgiveness.

At the conclusion of the evidence, and with no defence lawyers as was the custom at that time, the Judge summed up, adding that the evidence had been simply given and well presented. Then he addressed the jury.

'Members of the jury, you have heard the evidence in this case. I would point out that at no time has the defendant admitted his priesthood and the witnesses you have heard have not established that Nicholas Postgate was trained abroad or that he is a Jesuit or that he is a seminary priest or that he is a disobedient person contrary to the statute. There has been no evidence of him not taking the Oath of Supremacy, no evidence of him being ordered to leave England within forty days of arrival, or within three days of refusing to take the Oath of Supremacy.'

'All that we have heard is that he was reputedly a priest of Rome, that he baptised children, married couples, buried the dead and celebrated Mass in secret places. What you must decide on the evidence presented to this court, and only upon that evidence, is whether this man of eighty years or thereabouts is a traitor to the realm under a statute enacted almost a century ago. In accordance with Bushell's case of 1670, I cannot direct you. You and you alone must decide whether or not he is guilty.'

Later, a report of the trial in the *Gentleman's Magazine* described the judge as a red-coated huntsman crying the hounds to their prey, but this was untrue. The judge did his best for Father Postgate but the jury was determined to find him guilty. Before their verdict was announced, the judge addressed Father Postgate.

'Mr Postgate, is there anything you wish to say to members of the jury at this stage?'

'No, Your Honour, I would not wish to influence them in any way.'

'Thank you, so, members of the jury, I now ask you to retire to the jury room to consider your verdict. You may take as long as you feel necessary.'

And so they filed out. The judge and sheriff then left the courtroom as everyone else awaited the jury's return. Everyone sat in silence, although an usher came over to Father Postgate and whispered, 'I think the judge is on your side, Mr Postgate. That is a good omen.'

'Thank you for that thought.'

Then, after about fifteen minutes, it was announced that the jury had reached a decision. An usher shouted, 'The court will rise!'

Everyone rose to their feet as the judge and sheriff returned to take their seats, and then they all sat down. The jury was then asked to return to the courtroom.

In total silence, they filed back into their box and settled down. The judge addressed them. 'Members of the jury, have you reached a verdict?'

The foreman rose to his feet. 'Yes, Your Honour.'

'And do you all agree with that verdict?'

'Yes, Your Honour.'

'Then please inform the court.'

'We find the prisoner, Nicholas Postgate, guilty as charged.'

There were cries and shouts of incredulous disbelief as people in the public gallery responded to this decision. Someone shouted 'Silence in court!' as the judge rapped on his table with a gavel. 'Silence in court!' It took a few minutes for order to be restored, after which the judge said to Father Postgate, 'Please stand, Mr Postgate.' He did so.

'Nicholas Postgate, you have been found guilty of treason in that you are a priest of Rome trained overseas and now practising your religion in this country, contrary to the laws of England.' He halted, opened a drawer in his table and placed a nine inch square patch of black silk upon his head before continuing, 'The law of England states that traitors must suffer death and so it is the order of this court that you will be taken hence to the prison in which you were last confined and from there to a place of execution on a date to be determined, and there you will hang by the neck until your body is cut down, your entrails cut from your carcase, and your remains quartered as laid down by law. May the Lord have mercy upon your soul.'

'Dominus vobiscum,' replied Father Postgate, adding for the benefit of all, 'It means God be with you. And I thank you, Your Honour, for providing me with a short route to heaven.'

'As a special concession, Mr Postgate, you may receive visitors in York Castle prison as you await execution. That is my order. Now take him down,' said the judge.

An usher took Father Postgate's arm and led him back down the steps into the dark cell below from where he would be returned to York Castle to await his execution. Although it would occur on the Knavesmire at York, the date had not been fixed. When he was returned to his cell, he was left alone by his jailer to contemplate his fate, but, being a man of God, he was not afraid either of death or of dying. He had spent his entire life preparing for that moment, in whatever form it came, and he had also helped others with similar preparations, albeit with less violent means of meeting their Maker.

In those first few moments, he knelt and prayed the *De Profundis* from Psalm 130—'Out of the depths I have cried to Thee, O Lord, Lord hear my voice...' He followed the prayer with his own private Mass.

Later as he walked around the prison exercise yard, he realised that neither Luke Readman, Edmund Roe or Matthew Lyth had returned and so he occupied himself visiting other prisoners, comforting those who proclaimed their innocence and then his jailer hailed him. 'Mr Postgate,' said the jailer. 'You have a visitor. You may take her to your cell for privacy, if you wish. Your judge has ordered us to care for you and respect you. Clearly, you are someone important to him, so I must obey.'

His visitor was Elizabeth Baxter and she was sobbing as she walked towards him, wringing her hands.

'I had to come,' she said. 'I had no idea what I was doing to you, Father, no idea at all...I am so sorry, so dreadfully upset and mortified by all that has happened...'

'I forgive you, Elizabeth, after all, as I said before, you have done nothing but tell the truth. Who can be criticised for doing that?'

'But I testified against you, Father, against you! You of all people. That is unforgivable. You have always been so kind to me, so helpful...'

'I do forgive you,' and he made the sign of the cross before her as his form of blessing. 'I forgive you for this, and I forgive all your sins.

Elizabeth, I am an old man and am growing somewhat weary of life. These last years, walking those moors in all weathers has not been easy but I am not complaining. I am stating the truth, you see, and it has been my privilege to minister to my flock on those moors, like a shepherd tending his sheep against all the odds and in all weathers. Mine has been the work of God with Christ as my example, and I have been privileged to do so for more years than I care to remember. Now, I am an old man, my death from natural causes cannot be far ahead, and so this trial has speeded my end somewhat. I am not afraid to meet my Maker.'

He took her into his cell and they chatted for a long time with Elizabeth asking his blessing for her future life in Scarborough, and adding that she would always pray for him and remember him. She left after about half an hour and he watched her leave, still in tears. There was a tear in his eye too.

When Readman, Roe and Lyth returned, they told him they had also been found guilty of harbouring a Catholic priest, and all had been sentenced to a year in prison. The alternative had been a heavy fine.

'None of us could pay the fines, Father,' said Matthew Lyth. 'It would cripple us, we need money to run our farms, to buy cattle, pay wages and so forth. So we opted for prison. The year will soon pass, I hope our families can cope.'

'I'm sorry, I have brought this upon you.'

'Rubbish! Everyone of us volunteered to help you and provide you with accommodation, we have no regrets, and would do it again.'

'We can get out of prison, Father,' said Edmund Roe. 'If we apostatise and promise to attend Church of England services, our sentences will be cancelled.'

'We could always pretend to apostatise,' smiled Luke Readman. 'That might be one way of securing our release in time for the harvest. It is a thought. If that does happen, Father, rest assured we shall not go to Protestant services, it is just a ploy to get us out of here. Is that sinful, to use such deceit?'

'God alone could answer that, Luke and I am sure he will not punish you for such practical guile. I would not attempt to answer your question, simply saying the decision is entirely yours,' smiled the priest. 'Whatever you decide, I shall pray for you.'

And so the men of Eskdale settled down to prison routine with no date announced for Father Postgate's execution. However, news that a Catholic priest called Postgate was about to be martyred on the Knavesmire spread rapidly around York and the neighbouring district. This resulted in crowds of people making their way to York Castle Prison for a final blessing from the martyr-to-be; the judge's authorisation for Father Postgate to receive visitors was being amply demonstrated.

The outcome was that special times were set aside for him to receive the pilgrims, a large room being made available. He began to say Mass with an attendance of several dozen each day as the prison authorities ignored this blatant lawbreaking within their own walls.

In the early days of July, Father Postgate was having a conversation with the Governor when he asked,

'There seems to be a delay in announcing my execution? It is more than four months since my trial. It used to be the case that executions were carried out within days of a trial, even on the same day at times.'

'It's the same all over the country just now, Mr Postgate. Parliament seems reluctant to carry out such sentences, they acknowledge the falsity of the Oates Plot and the immense damage it has done. There is talk of Catholicism being once again permitted in England; after all, the King is known to be sympathetic, as well as other members of the royal family.'

'I am not really aware of the modern politics in this country,' smiled the priest. 'I've been too long out of contact with those in authority.'

'I agree that politics can be a dirty game, Mr Postgate, but from your point of view there have been no executions since 1654 with one exception in December last year. He was Edward Coleman, executed as a traitor at Tyburn in London. Perhaps you knew him?'

Father Postgate, realising the Governor had acknowledged his priesthood in the way he had addressed him, shook his head. 'Sorry, no, I don't recognise the name. So what happens now?'

'I am informed that Parliament is very unhappy about the number of priests who have been condemned to death and who are now lingering in prison, awaiting their fate, as you are. There is grave concern that most of them have done nothing to justify the dreadful penalties imposed upon them, mainly due to an old statute of Elizabeth being used to prosecute them.'

'So we wait even longer?'

'Yes we must. We have to wait until Parliament decides what to do. I have no authority to release you or to commute your sentence.'

And so Father Postgate, along with many other convicted priests around England, waited for Parliament to decide whether or not to hang, draw and quarter those currently lingering in prisons through the land. But on 11th July that year, 1679, the Privy Council issued its instructions. The Governor paid a sombre visit to Father Postgate.

'Mr Postgate, it is less than a week since we were discussing the lack of action by Parliament, and now all judges and prison governors have received orders from the Privy Council. The order, dated 11th July this year, refers to priests already in prison and awaiting execution in several counties of England. It says, "Their Lordships in Council have ordered that the respective judges who go on circuit where those priests remain must forthwith give directions that they be executed according to law." I am sorry, Mr Postgate, you don't deserve this, no-one does.'

'So is there a date for me?'

'Yes, Saturday the seventh of August this year. At the Knavesmire, it is along the Tadcaster Road that leads out of York.'

'Laus tibi Domine,' said Father Postgate with a faint smile on his face. It means 'Praise be to God.'

Notes

[1]   See p. 186, Father Postgate's hymn.

CHAPTER 13

Martyrdom

On the morning of his execution, Thursday, 7th August 1679, Father Postgate rose early, said his personal daily Mass and then spent the next hour or so in deep prayer. Apart from his jailer and a courtesy call by the prison Governor, he had two lady visitors. They were young Mrs Fairfax, the wife of Charles Fairfax of York, and young Mrs Meynell of Kilvington near Thirsk. Both were deeply distressed at his forthcoming fate, and because both were heavily pregnant they had come to seek his blessing before he was martyred. He placed his right hand upon the head of Mrs Fairfax and his left upon the head of Mrs Meynell, blessing each in the name of God and telling them, 'Be of good cheer, children. You will both be delivered of sons.' Some weeks later, his words were proven correct but both babies died in infancy, although they had been baptised.[1] Before they departed that morning, Father Postgate gave Mrs Fairfax his portable altar stone, and Mrs Meynell a pair of tiny candlesticks from his Mass kit.

They departed tearfully as the jailer arrived to announce that crowds were lining the route from the Castle to the Knavesmire via Ouse Bridge and Micklegate. Public executions were an excuse for a day out with stories to tell later with perhaps some trophy that could be sold for a profit. The clothing of martyrs, for example, brought good money as did their body parts and sections of the rope upon which they had died. Among the crowds there would be some nuisances but most were ordinary people who had come to bid farewell. A small number had waited outside the prison, to escort him all the way, some having travelled from Whitby and the moors with others from various parts of Yorkshire.

On York's Knavesmire, more than a mile from the city centre, executions of murderers, robbers, rapists and other criminal were quite frequent but the death of a Catholic priest/martyr had become less common.

Tears came to the old man's eyes, not because of fear but due to the faithfulness of his friends. 'I am dying for my faith and I will pray for them. I am beginning to feel like Christ on his way to be crucified. But I cannot match him for holiness and bravery. I am not afraid to die.'

He was wearing a new clerical suit, a present from some friends for 'his birthday in Heaven'.[2] It was an old custom that new clothing should be worn at one's execution—but Saint Thomas More had not followed this practice when he was martyred. He had retorted that the executioner would strut around in his suit afterwards! But Father Postgate also wore his favourite cross. Made of bone, it was the work of a child that had been given to him as a present. Proudly, he showed the cross to his jailer. On a string around his neck, it bore a rather crude drawing of Christ on the cross.

'You'll never keep that!' said the jailer. 'Someone will take it after you've departed this earth. And your new suit will be taken away by souvenir hunters too, Father, that's if the executioner doesn't get his hands on it.'

'I do not mind sharing my possessions, it happened to Christ also. It pleases me that my clothes and belongings can give comfort to others.'

'You are very generous. Come, they are waiting.'

Outside it was a hot and sunny August day with flies buzzing around and few clouds in the sky. In the prison yard, a horse-drawn sledge awaited. Father Postgate was ordered to lie on the sledge, on his back, and his arms and legs were then lashed to the woodwork.

There was no mattress and no cushioning, not even a handful of straw to make his final journey more comfortable over the rough road they were to take along Micklegate. A small grey horse stood between the shafts, ready to be given the word. A man was standing at the horse's head and holding its bridle, ready to walk it all the way to the Knavesmire. It was more than a mile distant, far beyond the city walls through Micklegate Bar and along the Tadcaster road. Someone gave the order to open the prison gates and so Father Postgate began his final journey, the sledge bumping and sliding along the route, hurting his thin body and bruising it in the fleshy parts. He did not grumble but coughed heavily in the dry air. As he passed from the confines of the prison, the crowd began to shout, some cheering, others jeering but many singing and praying aloud as the sombre procession passed by. Children ran beside the sledge, some trying to steal belongings from the living man but they were beaten back by the horseman's whip. Some threw ordure at Father Postgate such as rotten vegetables and horse dirt but his friends were on hand to protect him and remove such nastiness.

Among the crowd he noticed Tom and Dorothy Smith from Egton Bridge with several others from his home area and from various parts of Blackamoor; many of the women were weeping. Flowers were thrown too, these being plentiful during the height of summer, except for daffodils. They were his special flower but were now out of season. He hoped someone might plant daffodils on the Knavesmire after his death.

And so his long journey continued through a mixture of well-wishers, sight-seers and characters full of hate, as well as Catholics, Protestants and those of no faith whatsoever. There were people he knew and recognised from his many years of missionary work in Yorkshire, and there were total strangers.

As he passed through the noisy crowds, the people left their places and followed the sledge until, as they approached the

Knavesmire, the sledge was being followed by hundreds of people, many silent, some saying their prayers and reciting the rosary, other singing hymns and yet more simply running and shouting abuse. Some spat into Father Postgate's face and others spoke to him, doubtless seeking a blessing or wishing him well—they hoped he would be dead before the executioner began to remove his innards and cut apart his body. But that was doubtful—the method of hanging did not cause instant death and many such martyrs had witnessed their own innards being drawn from their bodies.

And then among the people he noticed as he crested The Mount outside York only a few furlongs from the Knavesmire was Elizabeth Baxter. Her sister was with her and both were weeping as they walked beside the sledge as it headed for the Knavesmire.

'God bless you both,' he called as their tears fell onto his old, dry skin.

'Father, no-one deserves this…'

At that stage, the authorities came forward and moved the women away from the sledge. They were turning onto the broad green acres of the Knavesmire where, in the distance, the scaffold was waiting with a crowd around it. The sheriff, as principal agent of the Crown, was duty bound to be present at all executions and he stood on the high wooden platform, waiting. Those who had accompanied the sledge through the town now ran forward to join the crowd around the scaffold. So great were the numbers that observers said Postgate's journey to the Knavesmire was more like a triumphant procession than the final trip for a very old priest from the remoteness of the moors.

The horseman forced his way through the outer edge of the crowd, using his loud voice and whip where necessary to clear a route and eventually he drew up behind the scaffold. Officials came forward to loosen Father Postgate's bonds, helping him to his feet and allowing time for his blood to circulate through his numbed and bruised limbs. He was then told to climb the wooden steps onto the high platform and stand below the noose; he needed help for that. His clothing was loosened and the noose was placed around his neck as he was made to stand upon a board marked with a white cross. It was a trap door. The noose was adjusted until it fitted snugly.

'If you want to address the crowd, Postgate, now is the time,' said the executioner. 'And don't make it too long.'

There was some jeering and throwing of rotting fruit and bad eggs, but shouts at the vandals by the crowd quickly ended that unpleasantness. Father Postgate, in a strong firm voice, began,

> 'Mr Sheriff, I do not die for the plot but for my Catholic religion. Be pleased to acquaint His Majesty that I have never offended him in any way. I pray God to give him His grace and the light of truth. I forgive all who have in any way wronged me and brought me to this death, and I desire the forgiveness of all the people.'

People were weeping and sobbing as some began to cheer as others sung hymns or murmured their prayers. Then the bolt was violently struck with a sledge hammer. The crash of the opening trap door and the dull thud of the dropping priest compelled everyone to lapse into a long deep silence that was quickly broken only by the sounds of sobbing.

The location of Father Postgate's grave is unknown although I recall one account indicating it was one day's journey from York. But it has never been found.

After bounty hunters had grabbed whatever they could by way of relics, the remains of his dismembered body were given to his friends who placed a brass plaque in his coffin. It read:

> Here lies the body of that reverend and pious divine, Doctor Nicholas Postgate who was educated at the English College at Douai. After he had laboured fifty years to the admirable benefit and conversion of hundreds of souls, he was at last

advanced to a glorious crown of martyrdom at the City of
York on the 7th August, 1679, having been a priest for 51
years, aged 82.

Even at that final moment, there are doubts about his precise age,
but reminders of his presence on the moors can still be seen,
including the Mass House at Egton, The Hermitage near Ugthorpe,
Red Barn near Littlebeck, the Mass Posts in houses and museums,
his relics and places listed in the following chapter. His old and
humble Hermitage now forms part of a newer building that uses
that same name. The Mass House is not the original either. In 1830
a space was discovered in the loft and it was still laid out ready for
Mass along with a cross, candles, vestments and altar vessels. Later,
the old house became in danger of collapse and so the present one
was re-built on the same site in 1928. During the work of demolition, a workman put his hand into the thatch and found a collection
of 17th century coins and a tiger-ware plate, evidently hastily
concealed. They were put on display in St Hedda's Church at Egton
Bridge but the coins were stolen in 1976. There is a small display
of relics in St Hedda's Church, including that collection plate. More
information about all the relics and places associated with Father
Postgate is given in Chapter 14.

On 3rd July 2011, a stained glass window bearing the windswept
image of Father Postgate was dedicated at St Hedda's in Egton
Bridge. The work of Thomas Denny, it was a gift from the Dowager
Marchioness of Normanby near Lythe.

But perhaps his greatest achievement can be seen in the people
of Egton and district who continue to revere him and his teachings.
The faith he lived and died for lives on.

After Father Postgate's conviction but before his execution, John
Reeves went to Thirsk Quarter Sessions on 29th April, 1679 to
collect his reward for apprehending Father Postgate. He was not
paid £20 as expected, but a mere £3 in florins. After receiving those

thirty pieces of silver, the wages of Judas for betraying Christ, Reeves is said to have committed suicide in the river at Littlebeck, very close to the site of Father Postgate's arrest. The pool became known Devil's Dump or Dead Man's Pool and local legend says no fish has since been caught there. However, there are fish in that beck—I have seen them—and it is interesting to note that there is no record of Reeves' death, no inquest was held upon his body and there is no known burial place. So did he commit suicide, did continue his career with HM Customs or did he return to London? In fact, he was reputedly seen after the trial in a public house at Pickering, accompanied by a small boy. Both were in an inner room enjoying refreshments.[3] Or did he survive to make his home in Yorkshire? Or could it be possible he suffered depression following his actions—even to the extent of joining a monastery to rebuilt his life and faith? His fate is an unanswered question, another mystery in the life of Father Nicholas Postgate.

Apparently, both Luke Readman and Edmund Roe apostatised so that they could get home to work on their farms but it is not known whether or not this was a genuine conversion to the Church of England or simply a ploy to get out of gaol.

Matthew Lyth was still in prison at York when Father Postgate was executed and apparently served his full sentence.

Descendants of all three still live in the area. I am proud that many of my friends and relations through blood or marriage are called Readman, Roe and Lyth, and the Watson family also lives in the district. Father Postgate is remembered in various ways but one is typically English—a pub at Egton Bridge is called The Postgate but the sign bearing his image has been removed. Its whereabouts are unknown—another mystery!

Following is the complete hymn reputedly composed by Father Postgate during his time in York Castle prison. It is known as Father Postgate's Hymn, and is regularly sung in Egton Bridge and Ugthorpe, particularly at funerals and at the Postgate Rally held every summer in one or other of those villages. Notable is his reference to the Five Wounds of Christ. As there is no proof that he wrote this hymn, both the words and the music in hymnals are usually credited to 'Anon.'

O Gracious God, O Saviour Sweet,
O Jesus think of me
And suffer me to kiss thy feet
Though late I come to Thee.

Behold, dear Lord, I come to Thee
With sorrow and with shame,
For when Thy bitter wounds I see,
I know I caused the same.

O Sweetest Lord, lend me the wings
Of faith and perfect love,
That I may fly from earthly things
And mount to Thee above.

For there is joy both true and fast
And no cause to lament,
But here is toil both first and last,
And cause oft to repent.

But now my soul doth hate the things
In which she took delight,
And unto Thee, O King of Kings,
Would fly with all her might.

But oh, the weight of flesh and blood,
Doth sore my soul detain;
Unless Thy Grace doth work, O Lord,
I rise and fall again.

And thus, O Lord, I fly about,
In weak and weary case,
And like the dove Noah sent out,
I find no resting place.

My weary wing, Sweet Jesus, mark,
And when thou thinkest best,
Stretch forth Thy hand out of the ark,
And take me to Thy rest.

The Postgate Society exists to further the cause of the Blessed
Nicholas Postgate and to promote the knowledge of local Catholic
history. It is based at St Hedda's Catholic Church, Egton Bridge,
Whitby, YO21 IUU. Members are always sought and encouraged
to continue the work he started.

Notes

1   Father David Quinlan, 'The Father Postgate Story' in *Whitby Gazette* (7
     April 1967).
2   *Ibid.*
3   *Ibid.*

CHAPTER 14

Father Postgate's Relics and Places of Interest to Pilgrims

AMPLEFORTH, NORTH YORKSHIRE

Ampleforth village is 20 miles north of York and four miles from Helmsley. It is readily accessible from the A170 Thirsk-Scarborough road and the Benedictine Abbey has a visitor centre and refreshments room. The Postgate Room is also available for small conferences and meetings.

St Laurence's Abbey and Ampleforth College, York, YO62 4EN

The following relics of Father Postgate are maintained at Ampleforth Abbey and may be viewed by appointment:

1. Father Postgate's hand wrapped in a cloth.
2. A simple crucifix with a crudely-drawn figure. It is made of bone and Father Postgate wore it at his execution. It has not been ascertained whether the bone is human or animal.

Some reports indicate that a piece of cloth dipped in Father Postgate's blood is kept at Ampleforth Abbey, but there is no knowledge of this. I have spoken to Abbot Patrick Barry (July 2011), the oldest member of the community, and he has no recollection of this cloth.

Further notes

An account in the CTS pamphlet *Ven. Nicholas Postgate (1928)* describes the Ampleforth Hand as the martyr's left hand with the thumb and forefinger missing. It was customary by the Protestant authorities to remove those parts of the hand because, during Mass, the Sacred Host was held there.

This relic was verified by Bishop Hogarth in 1853. Both the CTS pamphlet and Bede Camm's account in his *Forgotten Shrines* comment upon the paper containing this relic. It was inscribed in the handwriting of the period with the following (sic):

> This paper contains ye hand of ye Rev. Mr. Postgate priest who dy'd for his Faith, in suffering martyrdom at ye City of York Anno Domini 1680, togeather with a cloath that was diped in his blood. As alsoe certain very valluable and well attested Reliques of Saints. Therefore whoere thou art, be very careful of thy conduct herein.

There is a slight discrepancy in this inscription—Father Postgate's execution was in 1679, not 1680. It is thought that these relics came to Ampleforth Abbey through the courtesy of the Fairfax family, although it is difficult to understand why the hand should have travelled to Ampleforth from Hindley near Wigan in Lancashire.

However, it is known that Father Postgate's assistant, who took over his ministry of the moors upon his death was Father John Marsh whose family home was at Hindley. Marsh is a family name in that area but this Father John Marsh should not be confused with Father John Wall who used the name John Marsh whilst at Douai. Father John was executed at Worcester on 22nd August 1679, some two weeks after the martyrdom of Fr Postgate. It is possible that Fr Marsh of Hindley attended Father Postgate's execution and removed his hand for safe keeping. Whilst at Hindley the hand became an object of veneration, attracting pilgrims from Liverpool, Manchester, Wigan, Bolton and district but also from parts of the West Riding of Yorkshire. Not all were Catholics.

In records at the Lancashire County Record Office in Preston, there is a note about a cure associated with this hand. In her '*The Priest of the Moors*' Elizabeth Hamilton cites the entry as follows:

> June 24, 1851. Ann Cotton, N.R. Brownedge, Preston. St
> Vitus Dance. Protestant. Cured.

There was consternation at the first Postgate Rally at Egton Bridge
in 1974 when the two hands of Father Postgate (the other being
kept at St Cuthbert's Church, Old Elvet, Durham) were brought
together. Both appeared to be right hands, but because they were
so badly withered and damaged it was difficult to be certain. In fact,
a photograph of the Old Elvet hand in Bede Camm's *'Forgotten
Shrines'* suggests it is the left but photographs can be accidentally
printed in reverse as this one appears to be. The Durham hand is
undoubtedly a right, but the one at Ampleforth is difficult to
categorise due to its meagre remains. (See 'Durham').

COLWICH, STAFFORDSHIRE

St Mary's Abbey, Colwich, Staffordshire ST18 0UF

Father Postgate's relic, which can be viewed by appointment, is a
piece of flesh, or perhaps blood in a test tube, supposedly from his
executed body.

Further Notes

Relics of several English martyrs are in a locked case within the Abbey
Church. It used to be the custom to open the cabinet for veneration of
the relics on the Feast of the Martyrs of England and Wales (May 4) but
this practice has fallen into disuse.

DANBY CASTLE

Thomas Ward

The remains of Danby Castle stand in the Esk Valley between
Whitby and Guisborough. The controversial author, Thomas
Ward, was born here in 1652. He claimed to know Father Postgate
well, and the presence of a Mass Post, now hidden within the ruins

or perhaps in the adjoining farmhouse suggests the priest was a regular visitor. The ruin, once the seat of the Latimers, is now part of a working farm.

DOWNSIDE NEAR BATH, SOMERSET

Downside Abbey, Stratton-on-the-Forest, Bath, Somerset BA3 4RH

Father Postgate's relics, which may be visited by appointment, are scraps of blood-stained material. The relics are kept in a locked cupboard in a side chapel of the Abbey Church.

DURHAM

St Cuthbert's Church, Old Elvet, Durham DH1 3HL

Father Postgate's relic, which may be viewed by appointment, is his right hand.

Further Notes

The two locks of silky white hair tied crosswise in red silk reportedly at this location are no longer here. It is not known where they are, although a lock tied with red string or silk is in The Bar Convent at York. Father Postgate's lower jaw bone, formerly at Durham is now in the Church of English Martyrs, Dalton Terrace, York whilst his vertebrae is not at this church nor at English Martyrs in York. Its whereabouts are unknown.

Since the Postgate Rally of 1974, there has been uncertainty about the two alleged hands of Nicholas Postgate. The Durham hand is undoubtedly the right, not the left as suggested by a reversed photograph in Bede Camm's 'Forgotten Shrines.'

In 'Ven. Nicholas Postgate' (CTS 1928), it is described as the small *right* hand of an old man, the skin desiccated and brown. The little finger is missing and is said to be preserved in an unknown church. Portions of the skin have been pared down to the bone for relics, especially between the thumb and forefinger. The nails are intact and fingers contracted towards the thumb. Severed at the wrist, this relic was certified by Bishop Hogarth in 1853. The hand was formerly preserved at the English College, Douai and came to Durham following its transfer to Ushaw College.

EGTON AND EGTON BRIDGE NEAR WHITBY, NORTH YORKSHIRE

St Hedda's Church, Egton Bridge, Whitby, N. Yorks YO21 1UU

The long association between Father Postgate, Egton Bridge and Egton parish as a whole, has resulted in this church containing a large collection of relics and reminders of our martyr. The whole area is steeped in stories of his work and reminders of his presence, even though he was born hereabouts more than 400 years ago. Clearly, there is much to see and enjoy—and a lot to understand about his work and deep faith.

First, the relics in St Hedda's Church. The following is a list checked on 27th July 2011 by my son and me with the important co-operation of David Smallwood, a parishioner of St Hedda's who is Archivist for the Diocese of Middlesbrough. This list will differ from earlier accounts because some relics have disappeared or been transferred to other locations. Most of the following items are in the display unit at the church and can be viewed when the church is open.

1. Father Postgate's vestments recovered from the Mass House are *not* here. However, some pieces of fabric in a small box, one described as a piece of canvas and the other having the appearance of priest's vestment fabric, may have formed part of his vestments.

Also in this box is a button with what may be a button loop made of fabric in lieu of a button-hole.

2. A rosary that belonged to Father Postgate. It has five decades made from bone beads (although one bead is missing from the third decade) and it has a boss of leather. The crucifix on the rosary formerly belonged to Bishop John Briggs of Beverley who gave it to Canon Callebert of Egton Bridge who in turn donated it to St Hilda's Catholic Church at Whitby. It is now in this collection of relics.

3. The tabernacle door from the Mass House. This is surprisingly small and made of discoloured brass bearing a Crucifixion scene with Christ on the Cross accompanied by two sorrowful people in robes. They are thought to be the Virgin Mary and one of the apostles. In his '*Forgotten Shrines*', Bede Camm records how a well-known local Anglican clergyman dressed as a Catholic priest, visited old Mr Harrison at The Mass House, Egton and persuaded him to hand over the tabernacle door. It was missing for many years but eventually turned up at St Hilda's Catholic Church, Whitby and is now in St Hedda's at Egton Bridge. The Anglican clergyman died before publication of '*Forgotten Shrines*' in 1910.

4. The Pent House style roof of the tabernacle door from the Mass House. This is a triangular wooden structure but the accompanying frame is not thought to be the original.

5. Two portable altar stones

   i) Father Postgate's portable altar stone from the Mass House. After being discovered in the altar of the Mass House during the 1830 discoveries, this stone was retained (with the bishop's consent) by the Harrison family, tenants of the Mass House. In 1850, they gave it to the new chapel at Egton Bridge (now St Hedda's Catholic School), then in 1866-7 it was incorporated within the altar of the Blessed Sacrament Chapel (often called Lady Chapel) of the newly-built St Hedda's Church at Egton Bridge. The stone, approximately 6' x 6' x 1' is covered by a thick felt-type fabric that conceals its five crosses (one in each corner and one in the centre—the abbreviated symbol of the Five Wounds of Christ) but the stone does bear a handwritten notice that outlines its provenance. It reads 'An altar stone supposed to have belonged to the Revd. Father Postgate who was amongst the last Priests hanged at York for the cause of the Catholic Religion.'

ii) A second portable altar stone bearing five clearly marked crosses forming the X-shape is contained within the display at St Hedda's. It belonged to Father Postgate but otherwise its provenance is unknown.

iii) A third portable altar stone belonging to Father Postgate is on the altar of St Joseph's Church, Pickering. It is made from slate. This stone has a remarkable history—see the reference to Pickering.

6. Father Postgate's chair. This small armchair is made of wood and has a straight back and a rope seat. A non-Catholic lady told Father Toner, the parish priest of Egton Bridge, that it had belonged to her family for generations before being given to a Mr Turnbull of Whitby. The age and provenance of the chair has never been confirmed—it is claimed it came from either the Mass House or The Hermitage.

7. Stubs of two altar candles from the Mass House.

8. A ceramic tiger-ware collection plate, cracked and repaired. When it was first discovered it contained coins donated by the congregation at the Mass House. The coins dated from the reigns of Elizabeth I and Charles II. There were two half-crowns (now worth 12.5p), and the others comprised shillings (5p) and sixpences (2.5p) dating between 1562 and 1649. All were found hidden in the thatch of the Mass House during reconstruction in 1928. It is thought that the strips of waxed leather used to repair this dish were used by cobblers in shoe repairs. On 10th August 1928, an inquest decided that 22 of the coins should be returned to the finder, Mr G. Ward, with one (a mint half-crown from the reign of Charles II) being retained by HM Treasury as Treasure

Trove. Mr Ward later donated his coins to St Hedda's Church at Egton Bridge where they were on display but sadly in 1976 they were stolen. They have not been recovered.

9. Two pyx bags for carrying hosts to the sick. One is heart-shaped and made of old blue and white brocade with small flame-like tassels of yellow silk at intervals around the edges which are bordered with yellow silk braid. The second is made of green silk lined with red; it is heavily worn and badly frayed and was fastened at the neck with cord and tassels of green silk.

10. A small crucifix made of crystal and reputed to contain a relic of the True Cross; it now hangs on Fr Postgate's rosary.

11. A small book of moral theology written in Latin and containing Father Postgate's signature. This is one of very few examples of his bold handwriting. The book is *Aphorisimi Confessariorum* dating from 1599 and it was written by the Jesuit Emanuel Sa, published originally in Antwerp. This book was formerly in possession of the Bishop of Middlesbrough. Close examination of the artwork at the foot of Father Postgate's image in the stained glass window in St Hedda's will reveal the martyr's signature on the white page which is a representation of this book. He spelt his name as Postgayt.

12. A lock of Father Postgate's white hair in silver reliquary.

13. A scale model of the Mass House by George Harrison (1964).

14. A small wooden box inscribed TI ME DEUM 1585, 4'x 3'x 2', and probably used for carrying hosts for Mass, ie: as a travelling tabernacle. It can be opened and secured only by using a simple but effective locking system.

15. A piece of canvas with a button and button hole. This is not a complete garment and may have been part of a cloak.

16. A copy of Fr Postgate's hymn.

17. A metal heart-shaped locket bearing a Crown on the front, and on the rear 'LR' or 'IXXR'. As the letters I and J were inter-changeable c. 17th century, this may be a reference to King James II.

18. A very small piece of cloth, probably felt (approximately 2.5 cm x 3.7 cm) bearing an image of the Sacred Heart.

19. Two silver crucifixes—very small.

20. An oblong button, quite large and probably made of lead or silver.

21. A reliquary containing what purports to be a piece of the True Cross.

22. A wooden statue of what appears to be Father Postgate. Underneath its plinth are the words 'Ashtown Dublin. D. Sempers. St Anthony.'

23. A statue-like painted image of Father Postgate that is frequently reproduced in modern literature as an illustration.

24. Two tiny pieces of cloth. One appears to be bloodstained and bears the inscription 'La sanguine RRPP Shaving V Posket Ex sanginne' The second has an indecipherable Latin phrase and appears to carry a tiny piece of bone or perhaps part of a tooth. Their origins and purpose are not known.

Although many of these items came from the Mass House at Egton, it appears that some originated elsewhere and are not linked to Father Postgate. Furthermore, lots of small oak crosses of varying size and design are said to have been made from the wood of either the loft ladder of the Mass House, or the timbers of The Hermitage but in some cases their provenance is doubtful. They can be found in museums, churches and private houses.

Relics from the Mass House are listed in Bede Camm's *'Forgotten Shrines'*, the CTS pamphlet *'Ven. Nicholas Postgate'* and Elizabeth Hamilton's *'The Priest of the Moors.'* It appears that some candlesticks and an altar crucifix were given to the Harrison family of Scarborough, but have disappeared or been forgotten. The Harrisons of Glaisdale possessed a statue of Father Postgate thought to have been made from timbers of the Mass House. The sculptor is unknown. As Father David Quinlan wrote in the *Whitby Gazette* in February 1967, 'Relics (from the Mass House) were dispersed with regrettable profusion.' Many were later given to descendants of the Harrison family as presents on occasions such as baptisms, confirmations and weddings. Their whereabouts are unknown. Let us pray that some might be recovered to join those already in St Hedda's at Egton Bridge.

EVERINGHAM NEAR MARKET WEIGHTON, EAST RIDING OF YORKSHIRE

There are no known relics at Everingham, but see Chapter 4.

GROSMONT PRIORY NEAR WHITBY, NORTH RIDING OF YORKSHIRE

Nothing of this priory remains but when in its semi-demolished state, it was in regular use by priests returning to England from Douai, including Father Postgate. A farm on the site is known as Priory Farm.

HALSHAM NEAR WITHERNSEA, EAST RIDING OF YORKSHIRE

There are no known relics at Halsham but see Chapter 4.

THE HERMITAGE, UGTHORPE NEAR WHITBY, NORTH RIDING OF YORKSHIRE

Father Postgate's home at this site no longer exists but part of its wall was incorporated within the present building which bears this name. It is just off the A171 Whitby-Guisborough road near Ugthorpe. When the old house was demolished, some of its timbers were used for making small wooden crosses—they were widely distributed but their whereabouts have not been recorded. The name 'Hermitage' is misleading because Father Postgate was never a hermit. During his time there, it became known as Mr Postgate's or sometimes Postgate House.

KILVINGTON NEAR THIRSK, NORTH RIDING OF YORKSHIRE

There are no known relics at North or South Kilvington although there is a former chapel c.1690 which was built, apparently secretly, after the execution of Father Postgate. Dedicated to St Anne, it is on private property and sandwiched between two halves of a farmhouse. It stands only a very few yards from the site of Kilvington Hall where the martyr served as chaplain before his return to Blackamoor c. 1662/5. For more information about this chapel see Chapter 5.

LANCASHIRE

Lancashire County Record Office, Bow Lane, Preston, Lancashire PRI 2RE

In this record office there is a parchment-covered notebook that describes the building of the Catholic chapel in 1780 at Hindley near Wigan. It is not certain whether this became the present St Benedict's Catholic Church in Market Street, Hindley (in the WN 2 postcode district) or St Benedict's Church of the Sacred Heart, Swan Lane, Hindley Green, Lancashire. However, the notebook gave a list of *'Persons applying to be cured of their maladies by the touch of the Hand of the Revd. Nicholas Postgate.'* Some 200 entries were made between October 1850 and March 1853 which is more than 170 years after Father Postgate's martyrdom. It is not known why the people of Hindley had such a devotion to Father Postgate and we must ask whether Hindley's early Catholic chapel had any links with Fr John Marsh, Fr Postgate's successor. The Marsh family of Hindley were a recusant family.

Father Postgate's hand, now in Ampleforth Abbey, came from Hindley.

Stoneyhurst College, Clitheroe, Lancashire BB7 9PZ

Here, the relics of Father Postgate which may be viewed by appointment, are:

1. A piece of bone
2. Some blood-stained cloth

LOFTUS—NORTH RIDING OF YORKSHIRE

The Catholic Church of Ss. Joseph and Cuthbert contains an icon of Father Postgate on oak, also a stained glass window installed in 1987 and dedicated to Father Postgate. These can be viewed when the church is open.

MOORLAND ABOVE WHITBY, NORTH RIDING OF YORKSHIRE

Father Postgate knew the North York Moors as Blackamoor, a huge stretch of heathery open moors with stunning views that now forms most of the North York Moors National Park. The area was Father Postgate's open-air cathedral and is rich with opportunities for exploration.

Of limited interest is the Postgate Cross, a short stone pillar at MR 919044. This is near the junction of the A171 (Scarborough-Whitby road) and the B1416 to Sneaton and Ruswarp. Some reports suggest it is named after Father Postgate, and that he held meetings there, but that is doubtful. It is more likely to be a route marker.

The word *postgate* dates from the 13th century and means a route or track marked by posts to guide travellers. Postgate Farm at Glaisdale is similarly named and is not thought to be linked to the martyr, except that it contains a Mass Post. In bygone times, this farm was known as The Pilgrims' Inn due to the passage of pilgrims between Whitby Abbey and Rosedale Priory. It has an ancient custom of always being open to accommodate visitors.

Streets in northern towns and cities are often named as gates, eg Stonegate in York, Baxtergate in Whitby, Friargate in Richmond and many others.

OSCOTT, WARWICKSHIRE

The Museum of St Mary's College, Chester Road, Oscott, Sutton Coldfield, Warwickshire, West Midlands B73 5AA.

St Mary's College contains the relics of several martyrs, including those of Father Postgate as well as some recusant chalices of uncertain provenance. None can be positively linked to Father Postgate. The relics may be viewed as part of public guided tours at specific times. The Postgate relics are:

1. The cape worn by Father Postgate. This is a piece of linen stuffed with canvas with a button hole in one corner. It is described as 'Mr Poskett's cape he wore 30 years'. Folded in its display cabinet, it looks very small indeed.
2. A lock of silvery hair
3. A length of slender rope by which Fr Postgate was hanged.
4. Two pieces of bone, perhaps backbone.
5. Two pieces of linen, one stained with blood and the other clean.
6. A phial of Father Postgate's blood.

Further notes

The Oscott relics belonged to a pious lady called Mrs Juliana Dorrington who lived in Old Oscott and died there in 1731. She had been housekeeper to Fr Andrew Bromwich who was sentenced to death at Stafford on 13th August 1679, the last Catholic priest to be tried and condemned. However, he was not put to death and purchased the house from which the present college at Oscott has grown. He is the real founder of Oscott and almost certainly was acquainted with Father Postgate, perhaps through connections with the English College at Douai.

OSMOTHERLEY NEAR NORTHALLERTON, NORTH RIDING OF YORKSHIRE

The Monastery of Our Lady of Mount Grace, The Old Hall, 15, North End, Osmotherley, DL6 3BB and The Shrine of Our Lady of Mount Grace (The Lady Chapel), Ruebury Lane, Osmotherley DL6 3AP

Osmotherley is a large village on the western edge of the Cleveland Hills. It is a popular tourist resort especially at weekends and offers stunning view from the surrounding moors. One popular destination is Cod Beck Reservoir to the north of the village—it is locally known as The Sheepwash. The ruins of Mount Grace Priory are in the valley about a mile to the north-west of Osmotherley.

Sunday, 11th September 2011 marked the 50th anniversary of the re-building of the ancient shrine of Our Lady at Osmotherley. It is 200 feet above the ruins of Mount Grace Priory with access via a stony half-mile track leading from the road out of Osmotherley towards Swainby. That event took the place of the annual pilgrimage that marks the feast of the Assumption of the Blessed Virgin Mary—that pilgrimage is normally on the Sunday nearest her feast day on August 15.

The present Lady Chapel is not the original. Restoration began in 1959 after its ancient ruins were re-discovered by two young Catholic priests during a cycle ride from Middlesbrough. Its predecessor was the Lady Chapel of Mount Grace Priory, a magnificent and historic Carthusian foundation in the valley below.

One of only nine Carthusian houses in England, the Priory was founded in 1396 by Thomas Holland, the Duke of Surrey, Earl of Kent and nephew of King Richard II. He named the monastery the House of Mount Grace of Ingleby, and it was dedicated to The Virgin Mary and St Nicholas.

Its Lady Chapel was built in 1515 in the hills above the Priory less than 25 years before Mount Grace Priory was destroyed by Henry VIII's commissioners in 1539. There was a route from the Priory—it was a steep climb known as The Lady's Steps—and the Lady Chapel's grounds became the burial place for the monks and (possibly) for other Catholic martyrs - perhaps Margaret Clitherow. After Mount Grace Priory was dissolved, the Lady Chapel fell into disuse and there is no doubt it suffered during the Edwardine Visitations. Edward VI was the son of Henry VIII and the first English sovereign to be brought up as a Protestant.

He was only nine years old when he ascended the throne and, under the guidance of the Protestant arm of the Privy Council, he set about eradicating Catholicism from England. In 1538, among other restrictions, he issued injunctions that condemned 'wandering to pilgrimages', 'kissing of relics' and other 'such-like superstitions.' Edward stripped parish churches and chapels of all their Catholic artefacts such as statues, rood screens, the altar itself, wall paintings and prayers in Latin inscribed on the walls. He died when he was sixteen.

During the reign of James I (1603-25), it was said of the Lady Chapel at Osmotherley that '*the spot continued to be the goal of secret midnight pilgrimages by diverse and sundrie superstitious and popishly affected persons*' who visited the chapel especially on '*The Lady's and other saints' eves.*' In 1881, the Anglican Archbishop of York, Tobias Matthew, issued a writ in an attempt to prevent these night-time visits by people who '*arrived secretly and closely*' but it was ignored. Today, the Lady Chapel is widely used and Mass is celebrated every Saturday afternoon at 3.30pm and it is once again a venue for pilgrimages.

There has long been a Catholic presence in Osmotherley that was unbroken even during the Penal Times.

In 1650, at the height of the Catholic persecution, Lady Juliana Walmesley bought the Old Hall at Osmotherley where, in 1665, she invited the Franciscan Friars to create a priory there 'for the help and support of pilgrims.' More than 350 years later, that house is still used for that purpose although since 1994, when the Franciscans were having difficulties serving the parish, the monks of Ampleforth assumed responsibility for the Priory in the Old Hall. They care for the Lady Chapel too.

There is no doubt Father Postgate would have visited Osmotherley and nearby Upsall Castle particularly whilst he was the chaplain at Kilvington Hall. Importantly, he would have attended confession and received the sacraments from other priests.

The Queen Catherine Hotel at Osmotherley is said to be named after Catherine of Aragon, the first wife of King Henry VIII. It is thought to be the only hotel in England now named in her honour although other accounts suggest the Queen was Catherine Parr, his sixth and last wife who had links with the locality. Unless it was Catherine Howard, his 5th wife! See also Chapter 6.

There are no known relics of Father Postgate at Osmotherley.

PICKERING, NORTH RIDING OF YORKSHIRE

The Church of St Joseph, Potter Hill, Pickering

Pickering is a market town on the southern edge of the North York Moors and home of the North York Moors Heritage Steam Railway. Father Postgate was a regular visitor to the town. For celebrating Mass and accommodation he used a small cottage close to the Castle walls and said to be on the Whitby road, but its whereabouts are unknown. The Whitby road of his time is not the one in use today. One persistent story is that he pruned a pear tree in the grounds of his home but I could not find any record or surviving tradition relating to this tree.

Relics and reminders of Father Postgate, which may be viewed when the church is open, are:

1. A portable altar stone of slate, fastened to the current altar and formerly belonging to Father Postgate. The history of this stone is given below.

2. A copy of a painting of Father Postgate on loan from Whitby Museum.

3. A carved wood statue of Father Postgate, artist unknown.

Figure 5: Fr Postgate's Altar Stone, Catholic Church, Pickering

The Pickering altar stone

Prior to Vatican II, portable altar stones were used by travelling priests. About the size of a modern paperback book (6' x 9' x 1' or 15cm x 23cm x 2cm) and made of stone, say marble, slate or some other, they contained tiny relics of saints, perhaps a hair or strand of clothing. They were marked with five small crosses, one at each corner and one in the centre. These are the emblems of the Five Wounds of Christ. The requirement for priests to use altar stones ended with Vatican II.

Father Postgate's tiny congregation of only two at Pickering quickly grew and part of his legacy is one of his portable altar stones now displayed on the altar of this church. The stone has a fascinating history.

It was one he carried during his mission upon which to celebrate Holy Mass. It was given to him by Mrs Charles Fairfax of York who was a firm friend; she visited him when in York prison awaiting execution in 1678/9 and he returned the stone to her. Following his martyrdom, Mrs Fairfax gave the stone to Father John Knaresborough, author of many accounts of our martyrs; she also gave him a piece of cloth that had been dipped in Father Postgate's blood at his execution. Father Knaresborough then left the stone to Father Witham of Cadeby who in turn willed it to Father Thomas Daniel who gave it to a priest of Dodding Green near Kendal in Westmoreland.

Dodding Green has a long Catholic history, being a manor house that contained a secret chapel, priests' hiding place and escape route. It was used for daily mass throughout the Penal Times and continued to be used for Mass during the 20th century. There was a short period when the house was used as a second-hand book store and the celebration of Mass ceased but the house and chapel are today once again used by the Catholic Church. The building is now a place of refuge and safety for young people seeking to re-build their lives after addictions such as drugs or alcohol. It is now known as the 'Cenacolo Community, Our Lady, Queen of Martyrs', one of fifty such centres throughout the world and the first of its kind in the United Kingdom. When I discovered this story, I was concerned about the fate of Father Postgate's altar stone, but quickly learned that the stone had remained at Dodding Green until 1908 when it was donated, with conditions, to St Joseph's Catholic Church in Pickering.

Exactly what those conditions were is no longer known. According to Bede Camm in his *'Forgotten Shrines'*, Father Bryan of Pickering had long wished to have the altar stone for St Joseph's Church due to Father Postgate's association with the town, and so he was delighted to receive it. Bede Camm tells how it was let into the altar at Pickering, with his account being published in 1910.

Construction of the present church of St Joseph was begun in 1910 and completed in 1911, and so if Father Bryan let it into the first altar, it could have been a makeshift one in the temporary church that preceded St Joseph's. It is possible that it was later let into the altar of the new St Joseph's but removed when the high altar itself was re-ordered following the reforms of Vatican II.

There is no further record of the stone until 1986 or thereabouts when the then new parish priest of Pickering, Father Daniel McIver, found it in a box that had been made to accommodate golf balls. Father McIver had it framed in Helmsley and affixed it to the altar where it is now. He would detach it to take to the Postgate Rallies at Egton Bridge and Ugthorpe and Father Bill East, the present parish priest at St Joseph's (2011) continues to take it to Postgate Rallies where he places it solemnly upon the altar.

SAXTON NEAR TADCASTER, WEST RIDING OF YORK-SHIRE

Father Postgate's first chaplaincy upon his return from The English College at Douai was at Saxton Hall with the Hungate family. See Chapter 4.

STONOR PARK, OXFORDSHIRE

Stonor Park, Stonor, Henley-on-Thames, Oxon. RG9 6HF

It has often been stated (or rumoured) that there are some relics of Father Postgate at Stonor Park but my enquiries revealed that none is recorded there. Stonor Park is renowned for its association with the martyr Edmund Campion.

UGGLEBARNBY/LITTLEBECK   NEAR   WHITBY, NORTH YORKSHIRE

The following locations have associations with Father Postgate:

1. Red Barn Farm, sometimes known as Red Barns.
2. The stream known as Little Beck.

Further Notes

Father Postgate was arrested at Red Barn Farm on the road between Littlebeck village and Ugglebarnby near Sleights. When John Reeves arrested him, he found what were described as (sic) *popish books, relicks and wafers, and severall other things.* Undoubtedly, these would be seized as evidence for the trial and so their where-abouts are now unknown.

The farm house, which is private property, remains on its lofty site but has been greatly altered since that time. It is not known with any certainty which is the room where Father Postgate was arrested, if indeed that room still exists. The kitchen has often been suggested as the place where the arrest occurred. Red Barn is currently owned and occupied by a Catholic.

Little Beck is the name of the moorland stream that flows through the village of Littlebeck in fields below Red Barn. It joins Iburndale Beck before entering the River Esk at Sleights. Legend says that after John Reeves had prosecuted Father Postgate, he received 30 pieces of silver (Judas money - £3.00) but not his full rewards. Full of remorse for his actions, it is said he drowned himself in the stream at Littlebeck and it has been claimed that no fish have been caught in that beck since that time—Canon Callebert, the priest of Egton Bridge, is said to have put this theory to the test. With the owner of Red Barn and my son, we searched the river for indications of a pool deep enough to drown a fully-grown man but found few places where this could have occurred—however I did see some fish (minnows) in the river. It is said the pool where Reeves died became known as Devil's Dump.

As a postscript, there is no record of an inquest on the body of John Reeves and no record of his funeral or burial—see Chapter 13.

UGTHORPE NEAR WHITBY, NORTH YORKSHIRE

St Anne's Church, Ugthorpe, Whitby, N. Yorks

The following relics and reminders of Father Postgate can be seen in or near this Church; viewing of the relics in the church is by appointment, preferably during Mass times.

1. Two chalices
2. One paten
3. A watercolour painting of Father Postgate. It was painted in 1951 and was formerly kept in the Presbytery. It is now (2011) in the Church.

The white sheets said to have been used by Father Postgate to announce the location of Mass in this locality were kept at this church, but were stolen in the latter years of the 19th century. In or near the village of Ugthorpe are:

1. The Hermitage.
2. Ugthorpe Hall which had at least one priest's hiding place and where Mass was secretly celebrated.
3. Biggin House mentioned at Father Postgate's trial
4. Father Postgate's Well. His association with this well is unknown.

Further Notes

I visited this church on 11th March 2009 to view the two chalices and one paten. Almost certainly, one of the chalices was used by Father Postgate and the other is from the same period but with no firm evidence to link it with the martyr, although there is little doubt he could have used both. But there is some slight confusion about them. The smaller one was used by Father Postgate but that one does not unscrew to make it portable. It is said to be of French origin. Bede Camm in his *Forgotten Shrines* writes that St Anne's Church at Ugthorpe contains 'two chalices, both of which, probably, and one which was certainly, used by Father Postgate.'

More information comes from a paper in the Archaeological Journal (Vol. lxi, No. 241) by Mr T. M. Fallow, FSA, on 'Yorkshire Plate and Goldsmiths.' Mr Fallow writes, 'Both these chalices are interesting as having been those ordinarily used by the well-known Nicholas Postgate who at the age of 82 was barbarously hanged in York in 1679 for saying Mass. The smaller and apparently older chalice is a silver one of Gothic design with wavy flames around the bowl.' In fact, those 'flames' appear to be supporting the bowl on its stem.

The larger chalice (about nine inches/225mm tall) is said to be English and is thought to date from 1630. It bears fleur-de-lys designs around the base, an engraved crucifix and the initials Ora Pro D.M.F., (Pray For DMF). It was once thought they were the initials of Lady Charles Fairfax, a friend of the priest. However, her Christian name was Ann and she was Mrs Charles Fairfax, not Lady Fairfax. It is likely the initials may have belonged to, and the chalice presented by, a member of the Fairfax family.

It was customary in medieval times and long before the birth of Nicholas Postgate, for individuals to ensure their parish priest was always aware of their identity in case they died suddenly. To be constantly in the mind and prayers of the priest was important and so, to achieve that, wealthy parishioners would donate a chalice and inscribe it with their initials or name, perhaps on the lip or base. As the chalice was elevated at Mass during the consecration (also known as the sacring), it became a reminder of its donor at that critical moment. It was not, therefore, a personal gift to the priest but a vital *aide-memoir*.

At one time, the endorsed chalice at Ugthorpe belonged to Bishop Matthew Gibson, Vicar Apostolic of the Northern District and founder of Ushaw College.

For a time he lived in a house opposite St Anne's Church in Ugthorpe which eventually became the Catholic school. My mother taught there for a while and indeed it was a Catholic descendent of the Fairfax family (Mr J. Fairfax-Blakeborough) who encouraged me to become an author.

Young Lady Fairfax, accompanied by Mrs Meynell of Kilvington, visited Fr Postgate on the day of his execution. He gave to her one of his altar stones—the one now in Pickering Catholic Church.

There is no doubt the Fairfax family were strong supporters of Father Postgate and of the Catholic faith generally. It was a Mrs Fairfax of Gilling Castle near Helmsley who gave a house to the Benedictine monks to establish their school—it became Ample-forth Abbey and College, although the old house has been replaced by a new building. My wife's secretarial work was undertaken in that old house.

The larger chalice unscrews into three sections to make it portable and although it is fragile due to age and long use, it is still used on special occasions (and so is the smaller one). An account of the chalices appears in the CTS pamphlet *Ven. Nicholas Postgate* (1928) whilst Elizabeth Hamilton in her work *The Priest of the Moors* says, 'His chalice was used regularly at Ugthorpe until just before World War II when Father Currie, the priest at that time, decided to keep it for special occasions because the screw-thread was wearing and making the chalice unsteady; he did not want to have the three separate parts made into one.' It is felt the chalices are better in regular use in Fr Postgate's own country, than gathering dust in a museum. The paten at Ugthorpe was also used by Father Postgate.

For many years, it was believed the sheets hung out to announce the place of mass were kept at Ugthorpe. On 6th February 2009 I checked this with Fr Mulholland, the parish priest at that time but he had no knowledge of this story.

Certainly, no sheets from the period are now kept in the Church and further enquiries suggest they were stolen towards the end of the 19th century. However, when the first Postgate rally was held in 1974, white sheets were placed on the hedgerows to recreate that atmosphere but they were not original sheets from the Postgate era.

The Hermitage—see under Hermitage.

Ugthorpe Old Hall

In Father Postgate's time this was home of the Radcliffe family who had previously owned Mulgrave Castle. They were dedicated supporters of Catholicism who offered shelter and food for the priests coming into England from the continent.

Many arrived at Sandsend (then known as Sandyford) near Whitby and so Mulgrave Castle, with its farms, cottages and outbuildings, being conveniently near the shore, offered much-needed refuge and safety. However, the activities of the Radcliffes were widely known and members of the family were regularly fined either as recusants or for harbouring priests. In 1641, there is a record of William Radcliffe, gent, then of Ugthorpe, appearing before Quarter Sessions on a charge of recusancy, following the confiscation of his home, Mulgrave Castle.

His move to Ugthorpe occurred because he and his family were so frequently fined that eventually they could not pay and so Mulgrave Castle was seized by the authorities and in 1647 was 'dismantled' by the Protestant Government who had to use explosives to effect its demolition.

The Radcliffes moved into Ugthorpe Old Hall which dated from 1586. It had had at least one priest's hiding place and possibly two, one being in the out-buildings. At Ugthorpe, they promptly continued as before and converted one of the cow byres into a Catholic chapel complete with priest's hiding place.

Ugthorpe Old Hall is a listed building also known as Ugthorpe Hall, with Ugthorpe Old Hall Farm nearby.

There is now a modern Mulgrave Castle near Lythe, seat of the Marquis of Normanby and built by the Duchess of Buckingham in the 18th century, c. 1735. The remains of the two older Mulgrave Castles are in woodland below the current castle. The older one is said to have been built by a ferocious Saxon military leader called Wade before the Roman invasion, and the other dates to the 13th century. Both can be accessed by a footpath from Sandsend although the remains of Wade's ancient Castle are difficult to find.

It was the Dowager Marchioness of Normanby, the previous occupant of Mulgrave Castle, who in 2011 donated the stained glass Postgate window to St Hedda's Church in Egton Bridge.

USHAW COLLEGE, DURHAM

Because Ushaw College is the descendent of the English College at Douai, I felt it may have some relics of Father Postgate. Although the College has relics of three Douai martyrs, Henry Heath, Edmund Campion and Cuthbert Mayne, my enquiries revealed it does not possess any belonging to Nicholas Postgate. However, it does keep copies (not originals) of correspondence from 1707/8 between Ralph Postgate SJ, and Andrew Giffard. It is not known whether Ralph Postgate is from the same family as Nicholas, although Nicholas was thought to have had a nephew called Ralph who became a Jesuit priest.

Ushaw College ceased to be a priests' training establishment in the autumn of 2011 and its activities were transferred to St Mary's College, Oscott.

WHITBY, NORTH RIDING OF YORKSHIRE

St Hilda's Catholic Church, Bagdale, Whitby, N. Yorks YO21 1QS

Father Postgate's Rosary was formerly preserved here. It is now (2011) at St Hedda's Church, Egton Bridge. It is very likely that Father Postate visited Whitby at some stage of his life, if only to see the Abbey on top of the 199 steps. But there are no records of this.

WITCH POSTS OF THE NORTH YORK MOORS

I believe, thanks to supporting evidence, that these are not what folk lorists claim, namely they are not carved hearth-side posts that were used to deter witches. I am sure they were created in selected houses and farms around the North York Moor by Father Postgate and perhaps other priests. They provided a secret code that identified houses where Mass could be celebrated. See Chapter 7.

YARM-ON-TEES

The Church of SS Mary and Ramuald, High Street, Yarm TS15 9AA

A large oil painting of The Crucifixion formerly hung in the old Chapel of St Anne (1690) at North Kilvington. When the chapel was officially closed, the painting was taken to Yarm Catholic Church by members of the Meynell family who built the Church in Yarm. The location of the painting is unknown. Between c.1660 and 1662 or so, Father Postgate was chaplain to the Meynell family when they lived at North Kilvington Hall.

YORK

(1) Bar Convent Museum, 17, Blossom Street, York, YO24 1AQ

The Bar Convent is the oldest living convent in England, founded in 1686 as a school for Catholic girls—my three daughters were educated there. Now (2011) it offers accommodation for visitors, as well as a very popular café and museum of Christianity. It has a splendid secret chapel with a priest's hiding place and four well-equipped meeting rooms.

The following relics of Father Postgate are maintained here and may be viewed by prior arrangement. Relics of other martyrs are also kept here. Father Postgate's relics are:

1. A lock of silky white hair tied with red string, possibly silk.
2. A piece of rope by which he was hanged
3. One small cross made from the wood of the oak step-ladder leading into Fr Postgate's oratory at the Mass House, Egton.

Further notes

The Bar Convent also holds a pedlar vestment used during the recusant period especially by travelling priests but it is not known which priest used it. So far as is known, this has no links with Father Postgate. It is a 16th/17th century vestment with the stole, maniple and chalice veil as well as the chasuble. It is made of silk with stripes in all the liturgical colours—white, red, green, purple and black lining. It is very light and could appear to be a bundle of ribbons when folded in the pack of a priest who might be travelling disguised as a pedlar. It has been in the Bar Convent's collection for an unknown number of years. A similar vestment is kept at the Catholic church of St John the Evangelist at Easingwold between York and Thirsk.

(2) English Martyr's Church, Dalton Terrace, York YO24 4DA

This parish was founded in 1882 on the south of the River Ouse in York, then in the Diocese of Leeds. It is now part of the Diocese of Middlesbrough.

The following relics of Father Postgate are maintained here and may be visited in the shrine which is accessible when the church is open:

1. Father Postgate's jaw-bone minus all the teeth (This was formerly kept at St Cuthbert's Church, Old Elvet, Durham.)
2. A small wooden cross bearing a note 'From the ladder used by Father Postgate'—presumably from the Mass House at Egton.
3. Some reports suggest that one of Father Postgate's vertebrae is kept here, having been transferred from St Cuthbert's, Old Elvet in Durham, but there is no trace of it either here or in Durham.

(3) The Knavesmire, York

The Knavesmire is home to York Races and other events, including the Visit by Pope John Paul XXIII in May, 1982. This was the first visit to England by a reigning pope. A few hundred yards beyond the entrance from Tadcaster Road there is a small platform bearing a stone plinth. It bears the word TYBURN. This is a memorial to every martyr who was executed on The Knavesmire, including Father Postgate. It is known as The Tyburn Stone.

(4) A replica Mass Post

Chapter 7 of this book refers to Mass Posts, formerly known as Witch Posts. Somewhat curiously a miniature replica of such a post is carved into the woodwork of the bar at the Mount Royale Hotel which is close to the Tyburn Stone, English Martyr's Church and the Knavesmire.

It is the work of an unknown American woodcarver who, in 1981, was commissioned to renovate some timberwork in York Minster. The original post is in Quarry House Farm, Glaisdale but it is felt that the woodcarver knew nothing of Father Postgate but thought his work would avert evil in the hotel!

Whilst in York, do not ignore its other associations with Father Postgate—York Castle in which he was kept prisoner, the Guildhall in which he was tried at the Assizes and Micklegate along which he was dragged on a sleigh to his place of execution on the Knavesmire.

In addition to this list of relics and locations, I felt the following worthy of inclusion here.

A Mystery Crucifix

In February 2005, a priest called Father Kevin St. Aubyn was given a wooden crucifix (five and three quarters of an inch high—144mm) bearing a metal figure and the initials INRI. The donors were Mr and Mrs Martin and Patricia Keenan of Westbrook, Margate, Kent. The crucifix had been given to them by Mr John (Jack) Hill who was not a Catholic but whom they knew in Spain where Mr and Mrs Keenan had a villa. Martin and Patricia had helped Jack Hill and his wife, Babs, while in Spain. When Babs died, Jack was going through her belongings and found the crucifix which he gave to the Keenans because they were Catholics.

It had come down through the Hill family—but whether this was Jack's or Babs' is not known. Jack Hill had been the British Consul in Chile for many years and was considered a reliable and steady man. His sister, a Mrs Keeling, was still alive in 2005 when Fr Kevin received this cross. Reputedly, this crucifix belonged to Fr Postgate and he had it in his cell the night before he was executed.

A small piece of paper was glued to the back of the cross; it had an old appearance and bore some words, parts of which were missing, but 'Fr Postg Executed at York 7th Aug 1679' could be discerned. The paper has since been overlaid with Sellotape. The origins of this crucifix are unknown and its authenticity cannot be proved—but could it be the altar crucifix from the Mass House that was given to the Harrison family? None of the known accounts of Fr Postgate's final hours mention such a crucifix—the one he wore at his execution was made of bone and was much smaller that this one; that bone cross is now in Ampleforth Abbey.

This information was provided by Fr Dominique Minskip, then of the Postgate Society. It is hoped that someone may know more about this crucifix.

BIBLIOGRAPHY

Atkinson, J. C., *Forty Years on a Moorland Parish* (MacMillan, 1908).

Attwater, D., *The Penguin Dictionary of Saints* (Penguin Books, 1965).

Binns, J., *Yorkshire in the Civil Wars* (Blackthorn Press, 2004).

Bottomley, F., *Yorkshire Churches* (Alan Sutton, 1993).

Burke's Landed Gentry—The Ridings of York. 19th Edition 2005 (Burke's Peerage and Gentry UK Ltd).

Camm, B., *Forgotten Shrines* (Gracewing, 2004).

Duffy, E., *The Stripping of the Altars* (Yale University Press, Second edition, 2005).

Fletcher, J. S., *A Picturesque History of Yorkshire.* 3 Volumes (J.M. Dent and Co, 1900).

Ford, J., Some Reminiscences and Folk Lore of Danby Parish and District (Horne and Son, 1953).

Grainge, W., *The Vale of Mowbray, an account of Thirsk and its Neighbourhood* (Simpkin, Marshall and Co, 1859).

Hamilton, E., *The Priest of the Moors* (Darton, Longman and Todd, 1980).

Home, G., *The Evolution of an English Town: Pickering* (J. M. Dent 1905).

Jusserand, J. J., *English Warfaring Life in the Middle Ages* (Ernest Benn, 1889.; Methuen University Paperback, 1961).

Leyland, J., *The Yorkshire Coast and the Cleveland Hills and Dales* (Seely and Co, 1892).

Leys, M. D. R., *Catholics in England 1559–1829* (Longmans 1961).

Mee, A., *King's England series—Yorkshire East Riding and York City* (Caxton, 1950).

Mee, A., *King's England series—Yorkshire West Riding* (Caxton, 1950).

Mee, A., *King's England series—Yorkshire North Riding* (Hodder and Stoughton, 1970).

Morris, J. E., *The East Riding of Yorkshire* (Methuen and Co,1932).

Morris, J. E., *The North Riding of Yorkshire* (Methuen and Co. 1920).

Murray, J., *Handbook for Travellers in Yorkshire* (John Murray, 1874).

North Yorkshire County Records Office Publications 10/4 (1976).

North Yorkshire County Records Office Publications 7/3 (1976).

Northern Catholic History 51(2010) (North East Catholic History Society).

Peacock, E., *A List of Roman Catholics in the County of York in 1604* (1872, translated from the original MS in the Bodleian Library).

Pevsner, N., *The Buildings of England. Yorkshire, The North Riding* (Penguin Books, 1966).

Quinlan, D., 'The Father Postgate Story' (Whitby Gazette, 1967).

Rushton, J., *Yorkshire in the Reign of Elizabeth I* (Blackthorn Press, 2008)

Sharp, M., *The Traveller's Guide to Saints in Europe* (Hugh Evelyn, 1964).

Simpson, J. & Roud, S., *A Dictionary of English Folklore* (Oxford University Press, 2000)

Students of Ampleforth College, *Ampleforth Country* (1966 edition).

Ven. Nicholas Postgate (Catholic Truth Society pamphlet, 1928).

Ventress, M. P. , *A Little About Littlebeck* (Self-published, 2009).

Wilson, J. D., *Life in Shakespearean England* (Cambridge University Press, 1913).

INDEX

Helmsley Quarter Sessions 1615/16, 41, 42, 48
Hermitage, Ugthorpe 44, 89, 90, 91, 92, 128, 134, 138, 198, 210, 212
Herries, Baroness 49, 72
Hexham 71
High Treason—statute 164
Hindley, Lancashire 83, 190, 199
Hoby, Sir Thomas Posthumous 42, 122, 133
    Lady Margaret 42, 43
Holm 20
Holmwath 20
Horse Mire Head 21
Horseshoes, lucky 106
Houghton Tower, Lancashire 37
Hull 117
Hungate family 166
    Lady Jane 64–69, 82, 140, 166
    Sir William 64–69, 82, 166
Hutton–le–Hole 133
Hymn—Fr Postgate's 115, 129, l65, 185, 186

"I'll sing you One, Oh!" 115
Inglenook hearths 99 et seq, 108, 137

James I, King 42, 85, 203
Jesuits 4, 40, 54, 146, 164
Jonson, Ben 37, 39
Jowsie, Fr John 112, 159
Julian Calendar 9
Julius Caesar 9

Kilvington Castle/Hall 73–79, 80, 84, 111, 133, 140, 166, 199, 204, 215
    Bone relic 75
Kings
    Charles II 145, 152
    Edward VI 22, 70, 74, 135, 136, 205
    James I 42, 85, 203
    John of England 35
    Henry VII 119
    Henry VIII 35, 45, 85, 117, 124, 135, 136, 205
    Philip II of Spain 53, 54
    Richard II 205
Kirk 24
    Cliff 21, 26
    Dialect 24
Kirkbymoorside 18, 24, 137
Kirk Fields 26
Kirk, Low Intake 27
Kirk, William 95
Kirkdale viii, 2, 3, 4, 5, 6, 7, 18, 22, 24, 26, 86, 87, 89, 152
    Banks viii, 3, 4, 5, 6, 11, 16–18, 25, 26, 27, 39, 40, 87, 89, 152
    Cave 18
    Cottage 12
    House 3, 5, 6, 10, 12–16, 22
    Intake 27
    Minster 18, 137
    West Banks 5
Kirke Fields 26
Kirk–grim 27
Knavesmire, York viii, 57, 168, 179, 180, 181, 183, 216

228

Blessed Nicholas Postgate

Moors, North Yorkshire vii, viii, 32, 39, 88, 99, 101, 130, 200
Good Samaritan of the Moors 93
More, St Thomas 180
Morrice Richard 164, 167
Mortuary Chapel, Egton 6, 19, 20, 21, 22, 23, 24, 25, 27, 86, 123, 144
Mount Grace Priory 85, 202–3
Chapel of Our Lady 67, 82, 85, 202–3
Mulgrave Castle/s 33, 57, 90, 212, 213, 214
Estate 27, 213
Murder of Sir Edmund Berry Godfrey 146–151
Museums
Bar Convent, York 215, 216
Beck Isle, Pickering 135
Of Witchcraft, Cornwall 100
Pannett, Whitby 101, 110
Pitt Rivers, Oxford 101, 107, 133
Ryedale Folk, Hutton–le–Hole 101, 104, 105
St Mary's College, Oscott 7, 56, 62, 201, 214
Mush, Fr John 57
Mystery Crucifix 217, 218

Netherlands, Spanish 51
Newbiggin Hall 12
Newton–on–Rawcliffe 133, 134
New Year's Day 8, 9, 10, 82
Norfolk, Duchess of 72
Norfolk, Duke of 49

Normanby, Dowager Marchioness 15, 28, 184, 214
Normanby, Marquis of 213
North Yorkshire County Record Office 15
North York Moors Historic Steam Railway 135, 204
North York Moors National Park vii, viii, 32, 88, 99, 101, 113, 128, 200
Norton, Sir Richard 120, 129
Nunnington Hall 42
Nutter, Alice 112

Oak Bridge Holm 20, 21, 24, 25
Oates, Titus 84, 145, 146, 156, 158
Plot 84, 139, 145, 146, 153, 156, 158, 164
Ordnance Survey Maps 16, 17, 18, 23, 24, 26
Oscott, St Mary's College and Museum 7, 56, 62, 201, 214
Osmotherley 82, 84, 85, 202–3
Lady Chapel 67, 82, 85, 202–3
Monastery of Our Lady of Mount Grace 86, 202–3, 204
Mount Grace Priory 85, 202–3
Relic—Kilvington Chapel 75, 76
Shrine of Our Lady 82
Oxford, Pitt Rivers Museum 101, 107

Pannett Museum, Whitby 101
Papal Guard 138–140
Papal Visit, York 1982, 216